ParenTips

for Effective, Enjoyable Parenting

Best wishes!

Elaine Heffner

ParenTips

for *Effective, Enjoyable*
Parenting

by

Marilyn Heins, MD

Development Publications
P. O. Box 36748 · Tucson, Arizona 85740
520/575-7047 · 520/575-8586 FAX

ParenTips

for Effective, Enjoyable Parenting

For information contact: Development Publications, LLC
P. O. Box 36748
Tucson, Arizona 85740
Telephone: (520) 575-7047
FAX: (520) 575-8586
email: wlofquist@aol.com

Book and cover design by Richard Diffenderfer. Copy editing by Barbara Sears. Indexing by Wordability. Printing by Vaughan Printing.

ISBN 0–913951–06–4
Library of Congress Catalog Card Number: 99-74764

Printed in the United States of America

First Printing September, 1999

*For my children and grandchildren—with love
and gratitude for all you have taught me.*

Acknowledgements

My biggest debt is to the countless parents (and grandparents—and even the occasional child!) whose questions and comments sparked my search for answers. These nameless friends wrote letters to be answered in my parenting column, they called in to my radio show, they raised their hands at my workshops or lectures. They focused my attention on what today's parents are seeking and they taught me much about the problems of contemporary parenting.

This is the tenth anniversary of my association with *The Arizona Daily Star*. I am grateful that the Tucson morning paper took a chance on a rookie columnist starting out on a new career. I owe a special debt of gratitude to Bobbie Jo Buel, now Managing Editor of the newspaper, who was my first editor. And very warm thanks go to the present Accent Editor, Debbie Kornmiller, and Maria Parham who have become friends as well as colleagues.

I am also grateful to those who wrote to me after a column was published to take me to task because they disagreed with me or to suggest another viewpoint. The time they took to write spurred my thinking which helped me as I was preparing the manuscript. Many thanks to David Weintraub who parented me into the computer age and always responded when I cried. I am especially grateful to those who took the time and energy to review the draft manuscript, especially Judith Rich Harris, Dr. Vincent Fulginiti, and Dr. Alan Gelenberg. Publishers Bill and Mary Lofquist gave me support and encouragement every step of the way. Barbara Sears, Nan Badgett, and my sister Judith Leet provided me with expert editorial advice, and Richard Diffenderfer's design gave the book just exactly the look I wanted.

Finally, I lovingly thank my husband, Milton Lipson, for putting up with the birth of this book when he had already watched over the birth of our children and another book. His continued support and pride are the source of my strength.

MH

TABLE OF CONTENTS

ParenTips:

Parents' Fears and Worries

Contemporary Parenting Problems

Epilogue

x

About the Book

- Parenting is **NOT INSTINCTIVE!**

- Parenting requires **SKILLS** and **STRATEGIES.**

- Parents have to **LEARN** these **SKILLS** and **STRATEGIES.**

Sure, we were told parenting was the **most natural thing in the world—** put that baby into our arms and we'd automatically and spontaneously know what to do. **WRONG!**

What we thought was "instinctive" was learned. We learned how to parent by living in primate troops or human tribes where parenting skills were modeled for us. We lived all together then; now we are off in our separate spheres: our houses, schools, workplaces. And we don't learn much about parenting in school or college.

The other problem with this romanticized, inaccurate view of parenting is that parental "instincts" are supposed to be foolproof. We don't need intrusive advice from professionals. All we need to do is trust our "instincts." This worked when we were tribal because if one of our instincts wasn't right, another tribe member set us straight or took over.

Parenting is **not easy**—especially today. As a matter of fact I am absolutely convinced that it has never been tougher to be a parent.

Parents have never been busier. They have less time to parent and to interact with their children.

Never has there been more advice on parenting and less time to sort out conflicting opinions.

So, we have a dilemma. **Parenting must be learned and parents**

don't have much time to learn it. They need information but don't always have the time to read lengthy books or dig it out for themselves at the library or on the Internet. And they need professional information, solidly rooted in science and behavioral science, not anecdotal stuff that may lack validity and may actually be erroneous and/or harmful.

That's why I wrote **ParenTips**—*a new kind of parenting book.*

ParenTips takes a new approach to parenting advice and helps parents gain confidence in their parenting skills without taking precious time to read thick books.

This book has no traditional chapters. Instead there are forty-six ParenTips.

What is a ParenTip? A short "lesson" in the **skills** and **strategies** you need to solve the parenting problem or deal with the issue in the title of the ParenTip.

Each ParenTip starts with a list of **what to do** and **what not to do** followed by explanatory text. A traditional chapter is the reverse: text is followed by a summary or a box highlighting the important stuff. I put the important stuff **right up front**. If my advice makes sense to you, you may not even have to read the rest of the ParenTip—just follow the steps.

The ParenTips are organized into eight major topic sections, but each ParenTip stands alone. If you are having a problem with temper tantrums or wondering about what to do if your child has one someday, look the subject up in the index and go directly to that ParenTip.

This book is short enough so you can read it in one or two sittings. Or you can browse through an entire section. Or you can read ahead to an area you know is coming up like toilet-training, so you head in the right direction to prepare your child.

How did I decide what to include as a ParenTip? Actually, you—the parents—decided. As a parenting columnist for the Arizona Daily Star, I am asked many more questions than I can possibly answer. As a parenting educator I conduct workshops for parents and lecture to many different groups of parents. Because certain questions and topics recur frequently, it made sense to include the topics that most often concern parents.

This book is designed for busy parents so it will be of particular value to employed mothers and single parents—the busiest of all parents. But, because time is a precious commodity for all parents who live in today's complex world, the book is written for, and will be helpful to, all parents. It will also help grandparents learn about the challenges of contemporary parenting so they can be up-to-date in their thinking.

ParenTips is a distillation of all the wisdom about parenting I learned and wanted to pass on to my daughter when she said, "Mom, I'm pregnant!" Actually she said that four years ago and became the mother of twins.

ParenTips is a book of **skills** and **strategies**. It teaches parents what to do and what not to do, what's important and what isn't, and how to avoid making parenting mistakes.

ParenTips consists of **strategies** for parents that are **sensible**, **simple** to understand, and based on sound **science** whenever there is scientific data.

But this book is not a parenting bible. There are no fool-proof methods. I offer no guarantee that everything I say will work or is suitable for you, because no advice will work for every parent, every child, or every situation.

However, everything I say **I believe in.** And everything I say has worked in some, usually most, situations.

In one sense, this book is the opposite of a cookbook. In cooking you need to know a few basic strategies like do not dump the flour into the liquid all at once when making gravy. After you learn these strategies, you can follow the recipes and become a pretty good cook.

But children are more complicated than coq au vin. Raising children is challenging, frustrating and exhilarating because each child is different, each family constellation is different, each incident is different.

No parent would ever have time to read "recipes" of all possible situations in parenting. Nor could anyone write them all down.

There are some important strategies to learn about child rearing. And there are strategies for dealing with children in a loving constructive way. These strategies and the skills to carry them out make up this book.

When parents learn the **strategies of successful parenting**, they themselves can make the strategies particular. Parents can figure out their own techniques, based on these strategies, that will work in their own household. Parents can explain to child care workers what strategies are important in their household and why.

So, unlike the *Joy of Cooking,* this book has no recipes—though it has much sound advice. It provides you with road maps of the knowledge you need to figure out your own "recipes," to meet each parenting situation with confidence and understanding of both your child's needs and your own.

ParenTips is not a child care book. It does not teach you how to change a diaper or breast-feed or bathe your baby. It does not contain lists of approved car seats or toys appropriate for children of different ages.

Because **ParenTips** is minimalist, many parents will want additional information. *Suggested Further Readings* is an annotated list of parenting books which includes my favorite child care books as well as those parenting books that have helped me most in my parenting education work.

I know you want to do the very best job of parenting you possibly can. I trust you to incorporate the strategies and skills contained in these ParenTips into your own parenting in order to improve and enhance your parenting and the lives of your children.

Good luck and *Happy Parenting!*

About the Author

I am a pediatrician, mother, stepmother, and grandmother. In my professional life I have practiced pediatrics, directed a hospital pediatric department, and taught pediatrics to medical students and residents. I spent over twenty years in medical school administration, serving as the first woman associate dean at two medical schools before becoming the first vice dean at the University of Arizona College of Medicine. I wrote a parenting book and have written over 500 newspaper columns on parenting. I answered parenting questions on my own call-in parenting radio show and I have given numerous talks and workshops about parenting to diverse groups of parents, those about to become parents, grandparents, foster parents, and those who work with children.

In my personal life, I did what all mothers do: I worried a lot about how to parent! Parenting is something that nearly all of us do, few of us are educated or trained for, and all of us want to do the right way. The trouble is, almost none of us—and this includes pediatricians—know what "the right way" is.

I came to my interest in parenting education because of my interest in children, but now my main concern is parents. When I practiced pediatrics, I looked at parents as the caretakers of my patients, the children.

I now look at parents in the context of parenting. How can they find the skills and insights they need to parent in a world that no longer seems to care about its children? How do contemporary parents learn how to parent? Where do parents find the information and support that they need? How can they tell if they are doing a good job of parenting? How can I help parents in the parenting process?

To help answer these questions I have devoted the past ten years to parenting education dealing with parents in many different settings. Parents called in to my radio show with questions about parenting, they ask me questions at my workshops and lectures, they send more questions than I can answer to *The Arizona Daily Star* in Tucson, Arizona which publishes my weekly column on parenting. They even stop me at the supermarket to ask parenting questions!

I bring to parenting education my own experiences as a mother, step-mother, and grandmother. I can remember the struggles to do the right thing, the confusion about what the right thing was, the parenting mistakes I made which I will share with you in this book so you can learn from my mistakes.

My grown daughter, now a physician and mother herself, asked me jokingly "How come you're now a parenting expert? If I were grading you, I'd only give you a C-plus!" I silently thanked God I passed and answered, "I'm trying to help others learn from my parenting mistakes."

I well remember some of the parenting "errors" I made. Most of them were made out of ignorance. Yes, I was already a board-certified pediatrician when my children came along. But I was woefully ignorant about many important aspects of child development and behavior and just about all of the techniques of successful parenting. Pediatricians in those days were trained in disease, not development; bellyaches, not behavior.

Not only was I ignorant about kids, I was also pretty ignorant about myself. And those giving me advice—the children's pediatrician, for example—told me what to do for my children but never told me what to do for myself as a parent. Like many other mothers I thought my job was to pay attention to my children's needs. Nobody ever told me it was OK to pay attention to my own needs!

The bad news is that even a board-certified pediatrician may not know much about children and parenting. The good news is that parenting skills can be taught—and learned.

A parent doesn't need an advanced degree to learn the essentials. All you need is willingness to acknowledge that skills are needed in parenting—as in everything else we want to do well—and the willingness to learn these skills.

I try to help parents understand children and, almost as important, understand themselves. If I had known some of what I now know and if I had been taught what I am now teaching, I bet I could have raised my parenting grade to a solid B!

What Would I Do Differently?

If I had it to do all over again—

1. I would *learn about child behavior and development.* Parents don't have to commit to memory at what age the child develops the pincer movement of thumb and forefinger because you can always look it up. But you do need to understand the relationship of the child's needs and the parents' deeds to the developmental stage of the child. If I were parenting today I would use the knowledge of child development to **RELAX**. When you understand that the child will grow out of a stage, perspective is possible!

2. I would *look within* and learn to recognize what it feels like to be at the end of my rope. I now know there are two direct pathways to the end of one's rope. One is fatigue; the other, anger. Today I use the slogan, "Before You Explode or Drop, STOP!" to help parents realize that it isn't only children who need a time-out.

3. I would *take time to think.* Too often I spoke or acted hastily. I assigned a punishment that was too strict or I let a child off too easily because I engaged my mouth before my brain. Where is it written that a child needs an immediate answer to all questions? Some requests require deliberation or consultation. I would create a repertoire of temporizing comments like, "Hmm, I'll let you know later." or "Let me think about that."

4. I would concentrate on *enjoying parenting.* I enjoyed my children and cherished every moment I could spend with them. But I often worried about my clumsy ineptitude and my parenting errors. I brooded over what I did wrong yesterday and how my children were going to turn out tomorrow. Now I know that children are resilient and I understand the importance of *enjoying each day without worrying about yesterday or tomorrow.*

5. I would *slow down the pace of family life.* If your schedule is hectic on weekdays, have leisurely breakfasts on weekends. Take time to smell the roses—and teach your children how to slow down.

6. Finally I would perfect the art of **thinking like a child but acting like a grown-up.** I would have empathy for how small children feel when surrounded by bigger people constantly trying to make them do something or stop doing something. But I would always try to act like a grown-up imparting to the child I love, warmly yet without hesitation or apology, the greater knowledge and experience I possess.

Humbly I bring to parents my heart-felt empathy and understanding because I have walked in their shoes. I've been there. I understand what you are going through. I want to help. I sincerely hope this book—a product of my empathy and my professional expertise—**WILL** help you.

A Perspective on Parenting

What does it take to be a good day-to-day parent? What qualities do parents need in order to do their job?

The Parenting Job Description *includes having:*

- The ability to be responsible and postpone gratification.

- The ability and willingness to provide nurturing care to a child who needs it whether your child be a helpless creature, a sassy kid, or even an obnoxious teenager.

- The capacity to love and enjoy your children.

- The guts to be an in-charge parent.

- The ability to cope and be flexible.

- A passion to teach.

- Empathy.

- Patience.

- A sense of humor.

- Confidence in your self as parent which comprises both self-awareness and an understanding of the limits of parenting.

- A willingness to let go.

You also need a few basic skills to bring to parenting or learn on-the-job:

- Knowledge of children, including how they develop and their needs at different stages of their lives.

- Communication skills.

- How to control yourself and your temper.

- How to make a living.

- How to run a household.

- A willingness to reach for and accept professional help when you're stuck.

Parents Matter!

Parents definitely matter! Human infants, mammals who are born helpless, need care for many years until ready to take their place in our herd.

However the author of *The Nurture Assumption,* a recent publication generating much controversy, is absolutely right when she says parents don't matter as much as they think they do—and they don't matter as much as the "experts" tell them they do.

Judith Rich Harris stresses the importance of genes, which to a large degree determine temperament and personality, and peers in the ultimate outcome of parenting—how the kid turns out.

Although the nurture assumption—the assumption that nurture is what matters—is the basis of almost all of the psychology and parenting literature, Harris is right to point out that the basis for this assumption is very weak. No one has been able to show that a particular child-rearing practice or style or family structure (day care vs. stay-at-home mothering or gay parents vs. traditional family) predicts how the child will turn out.

Harris does more than debunk. She propounds a new theory to explain how kids turn out. The nurture assumption exaggerates the importance of parents while genes, though responsible for a good deal of personality and temperament, do not fully account for the kind of people children become.

The "group socialization theory" Harris proposes holds that "children's personalities are shaped and changed by the experiences they have while they are growing up." Yes children are born with certain genetically determined characteristics like personality but the environment can change them. Not the environment their parents provide but the one outside the home provided by peers (and to my way of thinking by non-relative adults, teachers/mentors, luck, etc.)

Many are howling on TV and in print that Harris is giving a dreadful message to parents. How can anyone in her right mind tell parents they don't matter at a time when child neglect and abuse are rampant?

What Harris says is that parents cannot change, nor even have much influence over, basic personality and temperament traits in their children. (Dr. Heins has been telling parents the same thing for years. I always get a laugh when I tell pregnant couples at childbirth education classes that the most influence they will ever have over their children is at the moment of conception and it's downhill from then on!)

For the sake of argument, let's assume *The Nurture Assumption* is correct: parents don't matter as much as they think they do.

Now what do "experts" like Dr. Heins do? Should we all find another line of work?

I am absolutely positively sure that parents today need lots of advice—advice that hopefully makes sense and does not add to the burden of parental guilt—for three reasons.

1. We're not trained for parenting and it sure ain't instinctive. Day-to-day parenting, like every other job, requires skills and strategies which can be taught.

2. It's a tough time to parent. Parenting today takes place in a complex, chaotic, crowded, competitive, consumeristic, confusing, rapidly changing world.

3. The nurture assumption has turned parents into frantic, guilt-ridden neurotics obsessing over the fact they didn't read to their kids last night.

Where Does All the Guilt Come From?

Parents I have talked to through the years seem to have two major worries: **1)** I will do something wrong that will have adverse and permanent effects on my child. **2)** I am not spending enough time with my kids.

Because of Worry #1 many parents seem frightened to discipline their children or even say, "No!" I call these "Parent Wimps".

For many years I wondered where all the fear and guilt was coming from. In the 80s, while researching the parenting literature for my earlier book, I found an article in "Psychology Today" written by Arlene Skolnick (February, 1978).

Skolnick pointed out that Americans are obsessed with, anxious, and guilt-ridden about parenting. Why? Because throughout the entire 20th century we have been bombarded with "expert" advice based on two conflicting theories of child-rearing.

On the one hand the Freudians warned us that the child is **vulnerable**, kids are delicate, easily damaged creatures. On the other hand the behaviorists told us that children are **malleable**, kids are blank slates with nothing written on them until they are molded by their parents.

Both schools of thought, though diametrically opposed politically and though proffering very different kinds of advice to parents, became the basis for what I call the "20th Century Parent Guilt Machine."

Both the Freudians and the behaviorists stress three things: **1)** Parents must do the right thing at the right time or their children will not become happy and successful adults. **2)** Parents can, if they only follow our advice, raise superior children who turn into superior adults. **3)** If something goes wrong and the kids don't turn out OK, guess who's to blame? It's the parents, stupid!

All of the advice based on these theories are part of the nurture assumption and completely overlook two very important points. Parenting is bi-directional— the kind of child that is born to you determines how you parent—and parents are not the only influence on their children.

The Nurture Assumption, by realistically clarifying the role of parents, should begin to chip away at this mountain of guilt and worry in which parents encase themselves. Guilt and worry are exhausting emotions that undercut the joy of parenting.

What CAN parents do that matters?

What can "experts" like me do to help parents?

I know that parents need **skills** and **strategies** to help them get through the day (and night).

Savvy parents will provide the following, not because they are obsessing about how their children will turn out or worried what others will think, but because **most kids will respond to, and do better with, this kind of daily parenting.**

- The three essential "Parenting Vitamin A's": **Affection** (it's more fun for you and the kids when you like them a lot). **Acceptance** (figure out and work with, not against, your child's temperament and personality because you ain't gonna change it). **Attention** (your children crave and need your individual, focused attention—not every minute of the day but some time during every day. And you need to pay attention to your kids so you can figure out what they are like and what they are learning from their peers).

- **Guilt-Free Parenting.** Do the best you can.

- **Joyful Parenting.** Read to your kids because it's fun, not because you worry that the Early Development Police are after you!

- **Skillful Parenting.** Learn the best way to help a child get over a tantrum today, without worrying about whether the kid will be an out-of-control adult tomorrow.

- **In-Charge Parenting.** Whether a toddler or a teen, every child needs to know the parents are in charge. Don't be a Parent Wimp!

- **Realistic Parenting.** Accept the fact that there are five things a parent can-not make children do: eat, fall asleep, poop, be happy, or turn out the way you dream they will. But you CAN confidently help them become grown-ups.

- **TODAY Parenting.** Stop anguishing over what you did wrong yesterday and stop worrying about how your kids will turn out tomorrow. **Just Parent Today!**

How your children will turn out is unknown. Harris told me that the notion that we can make our kids turn out the way we want is an illusion. "Love your kids because kids are lovable, not because you think they need it. Enjoy them. Teach them what you can. Relax. You can neither perfect them or ruin them. They are not yours to perfect or ruin: they belong to tomorrow."

Discipline

Basic Strategies

Learn to Talk Right!

Do No Harm

Master Five Useful Techniques

Basic Strategies

ParenTips:

- ### Respect Your Child.
  Validate feelings.
  Don't ridicule.
  Practice the Golden Rule.

- ### Model the Behavior You Want in Your Child.
  Give children "good" behavior to mimic.

- ### Remember You're the One in Charge!
  Don't be a **Parent Wimp!**
  Children are scared unless **someone's** in charge.

- ### Decide in Advance What's Important.
  Safety rules are always non-negotiable.
  Human feelings get high priority.

- ### Try to Be Consistent.
  Consistency never is absolute (people feel differently at different times and differ from each other). Reasonable consistency helps children make sense of the world.

- ### Use Your Child's Desire to Please You.
  Your approval is highly valued by your young child.

- **Give Choices Whenever Possible.**
  Minimize non-negotiable issues.
  Choices help future decision-making.

- **Encourage Responsibility in Your Child.**
  Start chores in toddlerhood.
  Add **responsibility** for chores in older children.

- **Try to Prevent Problems.**
  Read child's signals.
  Learn child's biorhythms.
  Use environmental control.
  Ignore, distract, remove.
  Teach child how to handle anger and stress.

I get more discipline questions from parents than all other questions combined. To set the stage for the specific ParenTips that follow let me deal with some general issues first.

Be Prepared!

Discipline is a difficult subject for most parents for three reasons. **1)** Kids don't come with owner's manuals. **2)** No two parents were ever raised exactly alike. **3)** Each family starts out anew trying to figure out the methods of discipline that both parents can be comfortable with.

Ideally, parents won't wait until the first playmate is bitten to start thinking about discipline. How early should parents start? Preferably before conception!

But it's never too late to sit down together and reminisce about how each of you was disciplined. How did you feel about it then? Now? How do you want to discipline your child today? How do you want your child to look back at *your* methods of discipline?

If you have differing ideas about discipline and different expectations about how you want to discipline the children, start adjudicating *now*. **Role-play** together, each alternating the role of the strict parent, the lenient one. Think of possible **scenarios** (Toddler Josh gets into Mom's brief case and makes an awful mess of her papers. Five-year-old Kate tells a bare-faced lie. Tom-the-Teen takes the car when he's told not to) and decide the best way to handle the problems. Keep at it until you both can be comfortable with the game plan.

Definition and Goals

What do we mean by discipline, anyway? Some of us think it means punishment. Some of us think it is a necessary evil that a child must experience to grow up civilized. Some see a noble connotation, as in self-discipline. Some hear an authoritarian word noting control.

My favorite dictionary defines the verb "to discipline" as "to train by instruction," and I find this a good definition for parents.

There are two goals of discipline: **1)** As parents we want to stop the child from doing something dangerous, hurtful, or annoying, which means the goal is to *control the child.* **2)** We also want to impart values which means the goal is to *teach the child.*

Compliance is what we want now, in the short term. For the long term, we want compliance to somehow metamorphose itself into self-control. But there is a difference between instant, unthinking obedience and thoughtful, insightful behavior.

There is an obvious conflict here, but most parents and kids muddle through! As children get bigger, we expect them to exhibit more self-control so we have to remind and chastise less often. And a child, who has by this time developed a conscience, can control his or her behavior with fewer reminders.

The first goal of compliance is impossible to realize in the preschooler who, regardless of what the parent says or does, is oppositional.

One study measured compliance in young kids and found it to be 40 to 60 percent. This means that, under the best conditions, preschoolers only do what we want them to do three-fifths of the time! (Galinsky, page 8)

Another study revealed that young children are asked to change their behavior—i.e., be compliant—once every six to eight minutes! Can you imagine how you would feel if your boss corrected you every six to eight minutes?

Because discipline needs to be defined and because the word doesn't come close to encompassing all of the things parents do in raising children, I use the word **socialization** a lot.

Socialization for me means *all of the processes parents use to help and guide* *their helpless infant along the road to mature adulthood.* It includes everything from the first eye contact which introduces the child to the human race to, "No you can't have the keys! No driving at night yet without our supervision."

The Development Factor

Behavior in a young child is largely *developmentally* determined. All parents know that a baby cannot walk at birth but can do so at around thirteen months. Parents understand that the child must be developmentally ready to walk before walking can happen. Developmental readiness for walking depends on myelination (formation of the sheath around nerves) of the nerves leading to the feet.

What parents sometimes do not understand is that certain behaviors such as reacting negatively to every suggestion are also developmentally determined.

If I had a magic wand I would wave it over new parents to instill in them both instant knowledge and instant understanding of the development of the young human mammal. But you can manage without magic by reading one or two books on child development. You do not have to learn the details of when children are able to do what. Just understand the **process** of development, realize the process is **innate,** and remember where to look something up when you need more information.

Discipline Is Your Job—Accept It!

Some parents want so much to please their children, to be their child's friend (Not!—you're the parent!) that they forget they have both the **right** and the **responsibility** to socialize the child so that he or she can become a functioning adult.

Some parents feel that it's their job is to make every moment of their child's life rosy and to eliminate all uncomfortable or unpleasant things in that child's life. These parents think, "If I'm just a clever enough parent, I'll figure out how to convince Sarah to let me dress her without a fuss!"

Sometimes we simply have to put the baby in the car seat and put up with crying because we must pick up the other children at school. We have no choice and the baby has no choice. Parents are a wonderful source of comfort for a child, but we don't have the power to *always* comfort a child. Nor can we always win a child over to our point of view or cajole a child to do what we want when we want.

Trouble can arise when children express their own feelings and try to exert their own will, independent of what the parent does. But, in addition, undesirable behaviors can be reinforced by the way the parents behave, especially parents who do not **feel** in charge.

Two types of reinforcement can occur. A parent may provide much too much attention to the misbehaving child. When you nag, shout, cajole, plead, or beg you are providing lots of attention—albeit negative attention.

Another type of reinforcement can occur with toddlers who are trying to figure out how much autonomy they can handle. If the parent is tentative in intent ("Should I really make Jonathan get in the car seat or should I stay home?"), smart children can sense this and turn the whole scene into a game called Make Mommy Change Her Mind. If the child wins a few times, the game will become part of that child's repertoire.

Socialization Takes Time!

Parents worry about how long it takes for the child to learn what is expected. "I have to say No! a million times—the baby won't listen (or doesn't learn)." Parents assume this means they have a future delinquent on their hands.

Not so. Children have lots on their mind because they are processing a huge amount of information that needs to be sorted out. Your baby is learning words, realizing that things come in different shapes and colors and textures, and recognizing that there are lots of different people in the world. Sometimes you forget where you put your car keys. Sometimes the toddler forgets the rule about no crayoning on the wall.

Do not expect that oppositional behavior in your young child will cease. It will diminish and you will learn to handle it better but it will not disappear because preschoolers must continue to try out their own ideas in order to learn that limits are a part of life.

The following strategies serve as the basic discipline course for parents.

Respect Your Child

I call "Respect thy children" the eleventh commandment. Oh that the world's children were all respected! They would all be born wanted, loved, provided with optimal nutrition, a good education, and an environment free from pollution and war.

Every child is a human being with feelings. Yes, your role as parent is to socialize the child, but becoming socialized requires learning on the part of the child and learning is greatly enhanced by feeling you are loved and respected.

Live and discipline by the Golden Rule. If you would not want to be ridiculed by your boss when he or she is correcting your performance, don't ridicule your child.

Model Behaviors You Want Your Child to Develop

Model those behaviors you want your child to have or learn.

Do you want your child to be courteous? Treat your child with courtesy. Do you want your child to be kind? Treat the child kindly. Parents are more powerful than they realize in shaping young children's behavior. And behavior is shaped even when parents are not consciously doing anything to modify the children's behavior. Kids are great mimics—give them good behaviors to mimic.

Remember You're the One in Charge!

One frantic mother I worked with complained, "I'm at the end of my rope with my three-year-old son. Yesterday when I wanted him to leave the bookstore in the mall, he screamed so loudly that I had to carry him out of the store. I'm never sure how to discipline him and I never feel I'm in charge. I realized the other day that I'm really afraid to take charge because of the reaction I will get. Is this what's called a power struggle?"

This *is* called a power struggle and Mommy *is* losing. But in the long run her son is the big loser.

Over the years I've met quite a few parents—mostly mothers, but some fathers—who were not comfortable in the parenting role, who had no confidence in their parenting skills, or who found it very difficult to discipline their children.

Some of these parents had low "parental self-esteem." They did not feel confident in their abilities to do many things—and disciplining children was only one of them.

Some had been treated harshly, or actually abused, by their parents and were so determined not to treat their children the way they had been treated that they overreacted and never corrected their child at all.

Some simply lacked parenting skills. These are usually first-time parents who didn't do much baby-sitting and are not sure which end of a child is up. They manage pretty well until the baby becomes a toddler. Toddlers are often tough to deal with because they are at a developmental stage when oppositional behavior is not only normal but necessary to their future development.

Some of these parents are mothers employed outside the home who feel guilty about their work status. They are reluctant to discipline the children because of their guilt. "How can I come down on the kids when I've deprived them of a mother at home all day long?"

Some parents believe that the child is vulnerable and will feel deprived of parental love if discipline is applied. Such misguided parents can be found trying to reason with a two-year-old.

It is vital that every young child knows the parent is in charge. The child has not been on the planet long enough to understand his or her own impulses and how to control them. The parent is the only and very necessary external source of control. If the parent won't or can't take charge, the preschooler thinks, "I am so powerful that even my parents are afraid. My impulses are the strongest in the world!"

This is terrifying to a young child who is aware of angry thoughts but doesn't yet know that wishes do not have to become actions and that impulses can be controlled.

All children need parents to socialize them so that they can one day take their own places in society.

The solution to becoming an "in-charge" parent is to look within and find out **about you.** If you need knowledge, take a parenting class or hit the library. If you lack self-esteem or confidence, get counseling. Then be **in charge.**

Do Decide What's Important

Decide in advance what is important. Safety rules and human feelings were the most important issues in my home.

Talk over with your spouse what is important in your family and discuss together what priorities to set about obedience and values.

Try to Be Consistent

I say "try" because consistency is an impossible goal to achieve.

The reason that consistency is pretty much a myth is that on the day we have a headache we may yell at the kids for making noise that we ignore at other times. Nobody is consistent all the time!

But reasonable consistency in oneself and between parents is worth struggling for because it lessens a child's confusion about trying to make sense of the world and figuring out how to do the right thing.

Use Your Child's Desire to Please You

Your child would rather have your approval than any toy on the market. Work with, not against, this desire to please. Be sure your child knows when you are pleased.

Give Choices Whenever Possible

Give choices whenever you can. This helps the child develop the ability to make decisions independently.

Start the choice process very early. What color shirt do you feel like wearing today? Shall we buy peas or beans for supper? And respect the child's choices, because this gives the healthy message that what the child wants **counts.** Never, on the other hand, give the child a choice when dealing with non-negotiable issues like safety.

Try to minimize the number of issues that are "non-negotiable" but never negotiate a non-negotiable issue. It's OK to let the child choose what color pants to wear, but it's not OK to let the child decide whether to get in the car seat.

Encourage Responsibility

Nobody can become mature without learning how to be responsible. Start chores in toddlerhood. Even a two-year-old can put folded clothes in the right drawer or put away the pots and pans. An older child should be expected to *assume responsibility* for chores, which means doing them without being told.

Try to Prevent Problems

Learn to **read your child's signals.** Recognize signs of fatigue, hunger, and over-stimulation and avoid these states that can lead to unwanted behaviors.

Learn your child's biorhythms and work with them, not against them. Crankiness and negative attention-getting behaviors often accompany hunger. Sometimes all that's needed is a "preventive" snack.

Children are affected by their environment. High noise levels can cause family tensions. Too many toys confuse and irritate children. Too many constraints make children angry—better to childproof the environment to maximize the degree of autonomy for your child that is consistent with safety. No need to have Aunt Susie's heirloom crystal where the child can reach it. No need to say, "Don't touch!" a hundred times an hour.

There are three time-honored preventive techniques that parents swear by. Use them!

1. Ignore mildly bad behavior. Most of it goes away. As a matter of fact it is more likely that a behavior will go away if you ignore it than if you call attention to it. Example: your two-year-old throws all the stuffed animals on the floor. No big deal.

2. Distract the child from bad behavior. The trick is to distract the child from what you know will cause a problem. Example: the baby starts to crawl toward an older sibling's puzzle. Use your imagination and have a repertoire of "distractions" that the baby likes to do.

3. Remove the child from a situation that will likely lead to bad behavior. If your toddler is heading toward your older child's model airplane project, remove the toddler **before** there's a crash.

Channel your child's behavior constructively. Your toddler likes to draw on the walls? Get an easel with lots of big sheets of newsprint.

Teach your child to deal with anger—the cause of "bad" behavior in most of us—and to manage stress. Give the child's feeling a name. Allow your child to express the **feeling** of anger although you cannot permit the child to act it out. Teach the child age-appropriate anger-reducing techniques like pounding a pillow or marching vigorously (with a drum if you can stand it!). Exercise helps all of us feel better. Older children can write angry thoughts on paper and then tear the paper into many little pieces. Children as young as two can learn stress reduction techniques (SEE PAGE 150).

I've given you lots of strategies. Discipline is a big issue so it takes lots of parental thought, time, and energy.

Don't get overwhelmed. Let me simplify it for you.

There are only three basic discipline strategies to learn.

1. **Prevent problems.**

2. **Talk right.**

3. **Do no harm.**

Understand these and master only five techniques to deal with misbehavior and you're all set—most of the time! Good luck!

Learn to Talk Right!

ParenTips:

- *Communicate Your Expectations Clearly.*

    Children are not mind readers.

    Early on, get in "parent propaganda" like, "We don't hit!"

- *Keep Your Voice Down!*

    Speak softly.

    Make 'em strain to hear you!

- *Do Not Talk Too Much!*

- *Use "No!" When You Must, but Avoid "No!" When You Can.*

- *Be Specific in Your Criticism.*

    Criticize the behavior, not the child.

- *Praise (and Reward) Good Behavior.*

    Be on the alert for good behavior.

    Be specific in your praise.

    Describe the good behavior, say how good it makes you feel, give child
    the word that describes it.

    Use "superpraise" — in front of another grown-up.

    Use all three kinds of rewards (social, material, activity).

- **Make Rules Specific and Understandable.**

  All rules must be:

  Specific and clear as a bell.

  Developmentally appropriate.

  Understandable.

  Enforceable.

  Brief! (too many words spoil the rule).

  No warnings! A rule should never be broken.

- **Master the "Effective Command."**

  Be **Close.**

  Be **Concise.**

  Start with **Child's Name.**

  Use a **Commanding** expression but speak softly.

  No need to say "please"—it's a command!

- **Use Humor—It Helps!**

- **Think Before You Speak!**

Communicate Your Expectations

State your expectations. Children are not mind readers.

Start early with what I call "parental propaganda" ("We don't hit!" or "We don't take toys away from other children!").

As the children grow older, your communicated expectations will get more explicit and more complex but should always be couched in terms the child can understand.

Expectations are not lectures or sermons. You are your kid's parent, not a professor or preacher.

Keep Your Voice Down!

Children tune you out when you yell or scream. Often the louder you talk the less attention children pay. The less attention the kids pay, the louder you yell until everybody is frazzled. There's a better way. Lower your voice. Speak so softly that your child strains to hear.

Alas, I was once a screamer but I changed my ways because of our parrot. One day I came home from work and yelled as I probably did most nights, "Rachel! Jeb! Pick up your coats! Put away your boots!" The parrot retorted with "Squawwk! Squawwk! Squawwk-squawwk!" imitating my tone exactly although not the words. I decided then and there that I was not going to sound like a raucous bird and cleaned up my act.

One trick: Remember that when you **feel** like screaming is precisely the time to take a deep breath and lower the decibels.

Don't Talk Too Much!

Avoid lengthy scoldings or tirades. The more you rant and rave, the less likely your child is to pay attention.

Try to keep all rules, effective commands, and disciplinary comments to ten or fewer words. "The rule is **No Hitting!**" is more effective than, "Big boys shouldn't hit their baby brothers. You're supposed to love your brother. I'll have to tell Daddy when he comes home. Blah-blah-blah-blah."

Unquestionably, brevity is better than a lecture or a sermon, so don't preach to your kids. But do have long talks with your children. When they become ready to debate issues, encourage debates over whether students should wear uniforms to school (general) rather than whether your children have to clean their rooms (specific).

Dialogue only works if you **listen when your children talk.** Model the listening courtesy you want when you talk.

Use "No!" When You Must

When you have to say "NO!" say it and mean it. Your child should understand from an early age that certain issues are **absolutely non-negotiable,** that parents are the ones who decide this, and nothing the child says or does will change your mind because you are the parent-in-charge. Example: buckling up in the car safety seat.

However, because parents **must** say "No!" hundreds of times, try to avoid the word whenever you can.

Try to "catch 'em being good." Then you can say, "Yes! Jody that was kind of you to give Grandma your seat!"

Turn things around so you can say "yes." Instead of saying, "No, it's too close to lunch for us to go to the park," say, "Yes, after lunch and nap we'll go to the park to play on the swings!"

Be Specific in Your Criticism

Criticize the behavior, not the child. "Hitting is wrong. The rule is no hitting!" is far better than "What a bad boy you are!"

Is this nit-picking semantics? I don't think so. Because children will do many "bad" things in the course of growing up and because your job is to call them on these, you might end up saying "bad boy" a zillion times before kindergarten. Your son could hear this so many times, he'd start to believe it. Better he think of himself as a good boy who did a bad thing and who will try to remember not to do that again.

Praise (and Reward) Good Behavior SPECIFICALLY

One of the most important things a parent can do is "catch 'em being good." Too often we only react to bad behavior.

Be a parent who is aware of what's going on and what your child is doing, not a passive parent who doesn't care what's happening as long as the kids are quiet. It only takes a minute to look in on the scene, recognize that the child is doing something good like cleaning up the toys, and briefly say that the behavior pleases you.

Always make an effort to praise good behavior and make your praise *specific*.

Specific praise comes in three parts: Describe what you are praising ("You put all your clothes away!), tell the child how you feel about what you just described ("I'm so glad you made your room look so nice before Grandma gets here!"), and give the child the word to describe it's action ("That's being responsible!").

It can be devastating to a child who, for example, cleans up the toys and gets no reaction or response from the parent. Your failure to respond invalidates the worthiness of the child's efforts and behavior.

Be specific in your praise. Not, "What a good boy you are!" but "You put all your toys away before Grandma came. That's being responsible!" Too frequent global praise can have a negative effect. In the first place, every child is well aware of not being good all the time. And second, if someone puts you on a pedestal, there's only one direction you can go, **down!**

Use the technique of "Superpraise" when you specifically praise the child in front of another adult. "Grandma, Sara cleaned up her room without being told because she knew you were coming to visit. That's being responsible! I'm proud of her!"

Sometimes a child deserves a reward for especially good behavior. There are three kinds of rewards: social rewards (a smile or hug, specific verbal praise), material rewards (cooking a special dish the child loves or buying a new book), and activity rewards (taking a trip to the zoo). All types of rewards work.

Make All Rules Specific and Understandable

Make rules *specific, developmentally appropriate, understandable, and enforceable.* In other words, clear as a bell.

Children need to know **exactly what you mean,** couched in terms they can understand. "Be nice!" is not specific enough for a young child. "We don't take other children's toys." is what you want to say.

Rules that are not enforceable ("Don't ever play with your brother again!") are confusing to children, as are threats that will never be carried out ("I'll never let you go outside again!").

After you introduce a rule or an expectation, ask the child to tell what was said to be sure there is no misunderstanding and that nothing got lost in the transmission from parent to kid.

No warnings! A rule is a rule. If you give warnings ("The next time you do that I'll———!") your message is that it's OK to break the rule at least once.

Master the Effective Command

When my children were small I didn't know any better so I used the most ineffective command there is: I yelled "Stop that!" from across the room.

When you need **obedience right now,** the operative phrase is, "Jody, get in your car seat!" Don't ask a question like, "Do you want to get in the car seat so we can go to the mall?" The child's logical answer might be, "I want to go to the mall but I'd rather sit in front with you!"

You don't even have to say "please." Please implies a request. A command is not a request. A command means Mommy *means* it. A command means, with apologies to Dr. Seuss, "I meant what I said and I said what I meant, Mommy's in charge one hundred percent!"

Don't raise your voice but do speak sternly. Parents who use these techniques tell me it actually helps to lower the volume of the voice while speaking very seriously.

Always be close to the child when you give an effective command. Get to the child's level (all those deep knee bends are good exercise!), touch the child, and make eye contact. Start the effective command with the child's name.

If the child protests, say "This is non-negotiable, Jody!" and repeat the effective command.

If the child will not cooperate, physically put the child in the car seat. Do not be upset by crying or kicking. As a matter of fact, try to tune it all out.

The crying will stop *provided you are firm in your resolve to do what has to be done and do not supply negative attention to your child's behavior.*

One role we have to play as parents is the role of autocrat. Let me make that even stronger. Sometimes we have to be dictators. We can't ever be brutal or abusive. We can't dictate every aspect of our child's life. But when it comes to an important issue, dictate we must.

We actually make things easier for our children if we accept this role with an understanding of its necessity and with conviction in carrying it out. *Dictate when we must and negotiate when we can is the model of good parenting.* It teaches our children important lessons about parenting. I remember hearing my daughter tell another five-year-old who was getting in our car, "Put your seat belt on right now or my Mommy won't start the car!"

In summary: to issue an effective command you must be **Close** to the child, always start with the **Child's Name,** make a **Clear** and **Concise** statement in a stern but quietly resolute voice, and put a **Commanding** expression on your face. "Andy, you may *not* hit Jesse with the truck!" No need to say please, it's not a request.

Use Humor

Use humor—and teach humor. Many situations can be defused by a good sense of humor. Learn to laugh at yourself. Capitalize on your children's keen sense of the ridiculous. Distract children by making them laugh. Families that laugh together are happier than those that are serious all the time.

Think Before You Speak!

Engage your brain before you engage your mouth. Almost every request from your child can be answered with a "Let me think about it."

Do No Harm!

- **Don't Spank.**

  Spanking message: It's OK for big people to hit little people.

  Spanking is not effective in the long run.

- **Don't Verbally Spank.**

  Put-downs, screaming, sarcasm, threats and nagging are all verbal spankings.

- **Don't Say the Child Is Bad, Just the Behavior.**

  Beware the rule of self-fulfilling prophecy.

- **Don't Compare Children.**

  Both favorable and unfavorable comparisons can be harmful.

- **Don't Assign Roles**

  Avoid phrases like, "He's the stubborn one!"

- **Don't Expect a Behavior Before the Child Is Ready.**

  Development is the key to child behavior.

- **Don't Model Unwanted Behavior.**

  A child's brain records like VCR tape—what your child saw you do could be there forever!

- ### *Don't Threaten to Withhold Your Love.*
  Terrifying to children.

- ### *Don't Be Afraid of Your Child.*
  Your child needs your courageous parenting.

Don't Spank

A basic parenting rule is do no harm. Spanking can do harm.

Spanking gives a bad message: It 's OK for big people to hit little people.

Spanking doesn't work very well. Spanking more often than not results in a child feeling hurt and/or angry and a parent feeling guilty. Hurt, anger and guilt are all bad states of mind for learning and learning is what discipline is all about.

Spanking hurts and there is a fine line between a "good" spanking and child abuse.

Spanking has a downside. Children who are treated violently sometimes turn into bullies themselves.

Let's face it. Spanking is violent behavior. If we want to decrease violence in our society, we must decrease violence in the home.

But I've never met a parent (including myself) who didn't admit to at least one swat. So if you have swatted, don't dwell guiltily on the matter. Adopt a more effective discipline method next time.

Don't VERBALLY Spank

I know many parents who wouldn't dream of spanking physically but they strike out verbally—and cause as much pain. "You dummy!"; "What a slob you are—there's food all over the table!"; "You're so clumsy you'll never be able to hit a ball!"

Be careful not to use put-downs when talking about a child ("Josh is so clumsy I don't think his father will ever be able to teach him to ride a bike!") because you are likely to be overheard.

Other forms of verbal spanking that should be avoided include threats, screaming and yelling, sarcasm, nagging. All these boring, repetitive unhealthy kinds of talk are counterproductive. Why don't they work? Because kids tune them out.

Don't Say the Child Is Bad, Just the Behavior

Children have a habit of becoming what they are called. You can end up in the thralls of just the self-fulfilling prophecy you most fear.

Don't Compare Children

Don't compare children either favorably or unfavorably. Avoid both types of comparisons: "Why can't you hang up your clothes as nicely as your brother does?" and "You're neater than your brother!" Deal with each child's behavior individually. Remember that comparisons are odious.

Don't Assign Roles

Avoid saying things like "He's a handful!" or "She's the lazy one!" or "You're stubborn just like your father!" If you do, your house could soon be full of self-fulfilled prophecies!

Don't Expect a Behavior Before the Child Is Ready

Don't expect a behavior before a child is developmentally ready. If you buy one book on parenting, make it a book that covers child development. Read ahead of your child's chronological age so you know what's coming.

Don't Model Unwanted Behavior

Don't ever exhibit a behavior you don't want your child to exhibit one day. Someone once reminded parents to think of their child's brain as a blank VCR tape on which everything the parent says or does can be stored forever. A frightening thought for all of us parents who regret something we said or did to our children. I certainly can remember wishing I had NOT done or said something in front of my children. Remembering the tape will help you realize the enormous influence we parents have on our children. Try to make your child's tape entertaining and instructive but not violent or X-rated for swearing!

Don't Threaten to Withhold Your Love

Don't ever say, "I don't—or won't—love you!" Children are terrified by the thought of losing their parents or their parents' love. The kind of love a child needs—and without which a child cannot thrive—is unconditional love. This means you love the child for his or her unique self and even for better or worse behavior. You love the child not for his or her appearance, attributes, or accomplishments but for the child's own self.

Don't Be Afraid of Your Child

Don't be afraid of your child or afraid of your role as disciplinarian. Never avoid legitimate correction of the child's behavior because you think this will somehow traumatize the child. Truly traumatized children are those whose parents have ignored them—have failed to correct them with love and understanding.

Master Five Useful Techniques
(That Work Most of the Time)

ParenTips:

- *Use "Time-Out" Correctly.*
    Time-out is opposed to time-in (attention from you).
    Select a boring place.
    Buy a special timer.
    Explain the process to the child.
    Allow one minute per year of age (child at least three).
    Keep young child in chair by hand on shoulder but don't talk.
    Repeat every time the behavior you are punishing occurs.

- *Use Logical Consequences.*
    Children need to learn their acts have consequences.
    Consequences can be natural or logical.

- *The Carrot.*
    Grandma's Rule
    Gold star charts
    Rewards for good behavior

- *The Stick.*
    Make the punishment fit the crime.
    Withhold privileges.

- ## *Ask the Child to Solve the Problem.*

  Have a meeting.

  State the problem.

  Ask the child what can be done to solve the problem.

  Stop talking and listen.

Use "Time-Out" Correctly

You can't use the time-out technique until you understand what "time-in" is. All children crave **attention. Negative attention will do if there's no positive attention at the moment.** Time-out is **time away from your attention.**

Prepare your child for time-out when the child is old enough. Age three is average. Some bright kids understand the concept at two-and-a-half but not much below that age.

Select the time-out place. The child's room is usually filled with toys and other distractions. Better to pick a really boring place like a dining room chair.

Buy a special time-out timer.

Explain to your child that from now on certain behaviors will result in a time-out. Show the child the place and the timer and show the child how the timer works.

Use one minute of time-out for each year of age. A three-year-old gets three minutes in the boring chair.

Scenario: Jimmy is hitting Jess over the head with a plastic shovel. You say: "Jimmy, hitting is not allowed. Time-out!" Escort Jimmy to the chair, set the timer, and **go away.** Ignore crying.

When the timer goes off say, "Time-out is over. The rule is no hitting!"

Repeat every time the intolerable behavior occurs. Be ultra-consistent.

If the young child will not stay in the chair, stay with him or her, placing your hand on a shoulder, but **do not talk or otherwise pay attention** or you will turn the occasion into a time-in.

With older children who are beginning to understand that behavior has consequences, you can give a Time-Out Warning if bad behavior threatens. "Jimmy the rule is no hitting! If you hit Jess you will be timed-out."

By the way, learn to take a *"Parental Time-Out"* when you need one. If you are heating up, leave the scene.

Not only does this prevent your yelling or doing something else you will regret but it models healthy behavior for your child. The child learns that when grown-ups get angry or upset, they go to their rooms to cool off. A good lesson.

My slogan for stressed parents, **Before You Explode or Drop, STOP!** With the exception of when a baby is in the bath, there is almost no time you cannot walk away when you need to. Put a baby in the crib or playpen, put an older child in his or her room, tell a teen-ager you need time-out and *go to your room.*

In each case the child may be unhappy. But better for the baby to cry until you are in control of yourself than be subjected to physical abuse or, what is more likely, be subjected to your screaming or over-reacting. Verbal abuse and seeing a parent out of control can be terrifying to a child.

Use Logical Consequences

Consequences can be natural—if the child smashes a toy, the toy is gone, the child can't play with it anymore. Though this consequence was a natural one, a misguided parent could ruin everything by replacing the toy. That would teach the child it's OK to be destructive.

Logical consequences are most often determined by the parent although sometimes it's a good idea to ask older children who have misbehaved what they think the punishment should be.

Responsibility depends on children's learning that their acts have consequences and that they are responsible for these acts. The parents' job is to help the child make connections between the behavior and the consequence. "Your green shirt will not be washed in time for the party. You did not put it in the laundry."

This means you should make every effort to make the punishment fit the crime. The consequence should make sense to the child because it IS logical.

Don't ever rescue a child from a consequence. Nothing is more counterproductive! Or less logical!

The Carrot

Everybody I know responds to **positive** rather than negative sanctions. Changing your behavior because you want to get something good means you are making a choice. You are thinking about the "good" you will get. You're in a good mood.

There has been some noise in the parenting literature recently to the effect that we reward kids too much and they therefore come to expect a reward rather than do the right thing because it's right. I suspect that this happens when parents do not use rewards correctly, or use them too often.

In my experience, thoughtfully used systems of rewards **do** work. The important thing to remember is that **unless the child does what is expected, NO REWARD!**

Grandma's Rule (if you do X, you will earn Y) is a time-honored way to get young children to modify behavior that is annoying but not punishable. "If you let Mommy dress you for preschool quickly, we'll have time to read the new book!"

Obviously you would not say, "If you stop hitting the baby with your truck, Mommy will buy you a bigger truck."

The old **gold star chart** also works. Children must be old enough to understand the system and be able to understand the concept of "future," which means at least three. I suggest you let the child help you make the chart with crayons. You can use symbols or pictures for children too young to read. With young children keep the period short—like a week of the expected behavior.

The reward should be small but desirable for young children. Activity rewards like a trip to the zoo work well. Example: "If you stay in your bedroom and play quietly in the morning until Mommy and Daddy's alarm clock goes off you will get a gold star on the chart. After a week of gold stars we'll take you to the zoo!"

This can also be used with older children who need motivation to do a task like taking out the trash without being reminded. Or to stop biting their nails.

You can also judiciously use an unexpected reward for good behavior. Yes, we expect children to be good when in a restaurant. But the first time a three-year-old sits quietly you can not only praise the behavior ("Sam, you did a good job keeping quiet in the restaurant.") but also reward it ("I'm so proud of you, I'm going to buy you a new book!")

Don't overdo this!

What should you do if Sam says, "Where's my book?" the next time he is good in the restaurant. Praise the good behavior and add, "We don't get a reward every time we do something good, only the first time."

The Stick

Children must also realize that certain behaviors will not be tolerated and sanctions will be applied.

Sanction rules:

- Make the punishment fit the crime.

- Be sure the child knows what the sanction is, and for what "crime" it will be applied.

- Apply the sanction consistently.

- Do not let the child's pleading or wheedling change your mind.

With young children, taking away toys can be effective. "Tommy, you tried to hit your sister with the truck. I am putting all your trucks away. Every time you use a toy to hit, I will take it away."

Withholding privileges works for older children. TV privileges or going to a friend's house are the ones used by most parents. "You did not clean up your room when I asked you to. No TV tonight."

Ask the Child to Solve the Problem

I get many questions from parents who are driven up the wall by a child's repetitive behavior which they cannot deal with. Nothing they have tried has worked—the child still sasses the parent or fights with another child.

One technique that works amazingly well is to ask the child to solve the problem. Children as young as five can often come up with a creative solution you never thought of.

Do the same thing you would do at work if you had a problem with a co-worker. You'd invite that person to lunch, state the problem, and ask what can be done to solve the problem.

Take your child out to lunch or breakfast—an away-from-home setting works best. One child at a time. State the problem. Add that you can't figure out what to do about the problem but you want it to be solved. Ask the child what he or she thinks can be done.

Here comes the hardest part: Stop talking! Wait for the child to come up with an idea.

Sometimes the child can't or won't say anything. Sometimes the child comes up with an unworkable solution. Children often suggest very strict punishments for themselves—"If I talk back to you put me in the basement for a year!" But more often than not a solution is proposed that works.

My favorite example: A not quite six-year-old kept hitting his baby brother who was almost fourteen-months-old. At lunch the mother said that this behavior must stop—"I can't spend all day putting you in time-out!"

When asked for a solution the boy thought for a minute and then said, "Put a gate across my door so the baby can't get in and spoil my games and puzzles." It worked!

Common Concerns

Sleep

Siblings

Self-Esteem

Toilet Topics: Basic Training,
Bed-Wetting

Sexuality/Gender

Sleep

- *Don't Let It Happen to You!*
  Most sleep problems caused by parents.

- *Be Sure Baby Is Awake When Put to Bed.*

- *Make Nights Boring and Darker Than Daytimes.*

- *Ignore Night Waking after Child No Longer Needs Night Feeding (Pat and Leave).*

- *Establish Bedtime Rituals Early*—quiet play to end the day.

- *Do Not Let Child Invade Your Bed.*

Sleep problems are quite common in early childhood and can be a source of great frustration to parents—as well as a cause of their own sleep deprivation. Although I hate to lay guilt trips on parents, they almost always cause these sleep problems by using loving, but misguided, methods to put babies to bed, namely letting the baby fall asleep in the parents' arms or in the parents' bed.

Children exhibit two common sleep problems: **1)** not going to sleep unless the parents are present and **2)** waking up in the night demanding parental attention before they go back to sleep again. In both instances the child has been trained to associate parental attention and touch with falling asleep. The parent is the child's sleep association.

We all have sleep associations—maybe turning over a favorite pillow or watching the ten o'clock news—but are not dependent on another person to fall asleep; we do it ourselves. In order to correct your child's sleep problem you will have to help the child develop his or her own sleep associations. You cannot make a child fall asleep; only the child can do that. But you can help the child learn how to do it.

One reason sleep problems are common is that parents were given advice that overemphasized the needs of the very young and totally helpless baby to develop a sense of trust in its needs being met. Thus parents were urged to pick up and meet the needs of a crying baby. This is correct advice, but advice-givers have not stressed the importance of the next phase of development when the child needs to build autonomy and begin to meet his or her own needs. Falling asleep alone is the first thing a baby can learn to do, long before being able to get food out of the cupboard.

I now make it clear to parents that babies should be put in their cribs **before they are asleep.** I still tell parents to pick up a crying baby. Just don't let the baby fall asleep in your arms. Continue to spend those wonderful moments cud-dling your sleepy baby in the rocking chair. But instead of letting the baby fall asleep in your arms or in your bed, learn the baby's signals that falling asleep is about to happen and put the drowsy infant down before that happens.

I remember how luscious it was to fall asleep with the baby in my bed after nursing, especially when the baby was very small. So I tell nursing mothers to enjoy this feeling but give themselves an age cutoff—say, three months—after which they nurse in the rocking chair and put the baby in the crib while still awake. Ditto for fathers who cherish the feel of the baby's limp, sleeping body. It's OK when the baby is very young but don't let it continue too long.

I also tell parents to train babies from an early age to learn the difference between night and day. When the baby cries at night, feed and change but don't play. Don't talk too much, keep the light in the room dim. This helps the baby realize that the world has both day and night and night is the time people sleep.

Night Waking

Sleep problems in young kids always mean sleep problems in their parents. It's rough to get up three or four times a night and still function the next day.

Night waking is one of the problems parents are always asking questions about, probably because it is so common until age four. Night waking is almost universal in newborns and during the first five months of age, after which it declines somewhat. To the great distress of parents, night waking often begins to increase at about nine months.

Between ages two and four night waking occurs in as many as a third of all children. This means one out of three sets of parents are sleep-deprived. It's tough on all families but can be devastating when both parents work and have to be out of the house early the next morning.

What do I recommend for a baby who wakes up crying at night but is not hungry? What about the toddler who has not needed a night bottle for over a year but still wakes up and wants to be held?

Try **systematic ignoring.** This means that parents just ignore the crying. The parent can look in on the child to make sure nothing is wrong but does not handle, feed, soothe, or indeed do *anything* that the child might use to reinforce this habit of night crying.

How do you play the systematic ignoring game? When the child awakes during the night, respond briefly (and be as boring as you can) at increasingly longer intervals. Keep a chart so you will remember whether you let Jennifer cry five or eight minutes last night. Increase the ignoring time every night until she is able to fall asleep on her own.

The advantage of using this gradual process instead of letting the child undergo the "cold turkey" type of parental ignoring is that it provides parental support while the child is learning how to fall asleep alone but also avoids leaving the child alone for long periods of time which adds to both the parents' and child's anxiety.

In the beginning the crying may get worse. Parents may feel increasingly guilty that they are not meeting their child's needs. However studies have shown that systematic ignoring works, does not have any bad effects, and actually may help prevent insomnia in adult life. We are beginning to learn that children who are allowed to and encouraged to develop their own sleep associations have fewer sleep problems later on.

There are other tricks parents can use. Get a new stuffed animal or doll and tell the child this is a Magic Sleep Animal. "Every time you wake up you can hug it and it will help you get back to sleep!" If the child seems afraid of the dark, use a night-light. Some children like a radio or tape recorder they can turn on by themselves.

Loving parents who continue to intervene every time their child cries at night are telling the child to expect parental comfort when it is no longer appropriate or needed. This retards the child's ability to learn how to self-comfort.

Remedial Measures

What if you're a parent who wasn't told this and now your child has a sleep problem? You have some work ahead of you, and you will definitely hear some crying and protestations, but the problem can be solved.

You must now help your child develop personal sleep associations and give up being dependent on your presence or body to fall asleep.

If you have a child who has never learned how to fall asleep alone in a crib or bed, your task is simple: Put the child to bed after a warm hug which will signal an end to the bedtime ritual. Say, "Good Night! I love you! I'll see you in the morning!" and leave the room.

No doubt the child who is used to falling asleep in your arms or your bed will protest. Dr. Richard Ferber, who directs the Center for Pediatric Sleep Disorders at Children's Hospital in Boston, suggests you let the child cry for five minutes or so the first night. After five minutes, go into the child's room to reassure the child that you still care, but don't pick up the child or go back to the old ways. Instead leave the room as you did in the beginning with a bright "Good night!"

If the child cries a second time, wait ten minutes before going in for the brief reassurance session. After a third time, wait fifteen minutes but don't increase the time beyond fifteen minutes on the first night. The object is for the child to fall asleep during one of the periods you are out of the room. If necessary, continue this routine until morning. Most children fall asleep on their own within a few hours. On successive nights parents should increase all times by five minutes.

Most children are falling asleep on their own within seven days. Several parents have told me that even though their child never fell asleep the first night, on each succeeding night there was less protest. Many children stop crying and merely whimper for shorter and shorter periods until they fall asleep. And when they awaken during the night they fall back to sleep on their own, perhaps after a bit of whimpering at the beginning.

Similar routines can be carried out for the child who sleeps in your bed or crawls out of bed to join you. You say, "You must stay in your own bed." If this doesn't work, close the child's door (you may have to stand against it so the child can't push it open). If the child gets out of bed, put the child back into the bed and close the door. Keep it closed for one minute. Then start the process again, increasing the time the door stays closed when the child gets out of bed by one minute up to five minutes the first night. The object of this routine is to teach the child that he or she determines whether the door stays open by staying in bed.

The nice thing about Dr. Ferber's method is that the child receives reassurance after only a brief period of parental deprivation—and the parents are reassured that the child is really all right, despite the tears.

These routines *do* work. They require a great deal of parental effort and may involve some sleepless nights. You also will have to warn your neighbors that the baby is likely to do some heavy-duty crying! But wouldn't you rather have one or two sleepless nights than years of habitual night crying?

Bedtime Rituals

Let's think about why a young child resists going to bed. Bed means separation from both the action (play) and the parents. These days when parents are out of the home a great deal children want as much parental time as possible and do all they can to get it.

Some children may be afraid of the dark (which really means fear of the thoughts that occur when we are in the dark) or of being alone. Others have difficulty falling asleep either because they are temperamentally poor sleepers, want to avoid bad dreams, or because they have never developed sleep associations on their own and really don't know **how to fall asleep** unless the parent is there with them.

Let's think about how parents feel. It's the end of a long day. The last thing parents want is a fight over bedtime. Parents are tired; they want some rest as well as some self-time and couple-time **without the children**. This, of course, can make parents feel guilty and even ambivalent about their efforts to get the children to bed. And some parents identify with their child and relive their own childhood sleep issues.

Before I get to the strategies, let me state a basic reality: **It is not in your power to make your child fall asleep. All you can do is set up facilitating conditions.**

● Establish a bedtime routine. Example: pajamas, brush teeth, toilet, hop in bed, Mommy or Daddy reads a story. Keep the ritual fairly simple so that when the child insists on every step you can do it without resentment!

- Make bedtime a special time of special closeness with the parents so the child will look forward to it.

- Keep the hour before the pre-bedtime ritual a time for quiet play—board games rather than jumping games. In our home I would put both children and a big book of folk songs on my lap in the rocking chair. We sang together starting with lively songs and ending with quiet ones.

- Encourage independence by placing by the bed a sturdy lamp that children can turn on by themselves if they are unhappy in the dark. Alternatively a nightlight or a dimmer switch can be helpful. A radio is also a good idea. Teach the child how to keep the volume low because "It's a **personal** radio for your ears only."

  Teach your children that falling asleep takes time. Tell them to think quiet or sleepy thoughts. If they are not sleepy, suggest they stay in bed and read or listen to the radio.

- Give the reluctant-to-go-to-bed child an early-warning signal. Some parents use an alarm clock set to ring fifteen minutes before the bedtime ritual should begin.

- Some children are relaxed by a bath at bedtime—mine were—but others are stimulated by playing in the water and are best bathed at a time other than bedtime. Some parents do the bath-and-pajama routine about an hour before bedtime, followed by quiet play or a snack and then the rest of the ritual.

- If the child still takes a long nap during the day, gradually decrease nap time so the child will be more sleepy at night.

- Don't yell, threaten, cajole, or beg. **Just be quietly firm.**

How Much Sleep?

How much sleep do children need? There is a good deal of variability in how much sleep an individual child needs. There are great differences in sleep requirements and patterns in adults as well.

The world seems to be divided into night people and day people. Children will sort themselves into "owls" and "larks," regardless of whether their parents put them to bed early or not. Sleep biorhythms are generally established in child-hood and remain for life.

Newborns need more sleep than toddlers who, in turn, need more sleep than school-age children. The average newborn sleeps more than 16 hours a day with a range of from 11 to 23 hours. By age two a child can manage with 12 hours a night, but needs a nap for an hour or so during the day. By the time the child enters school, about 11 hours a night suffices and this will drop to10 hours a night by about age ten.

The best way to find out if your child is getting enough sleep is to observe the child. Babies who are not getting enough sleep are generally irritable, fussy, or cranky—words that all indicate that the baby feels miserable and out-of-sorts.

Older children who are sleep-deprived may exhibit hyperactivity in the sense that they are more active than usual but also more disorganized in their behavior. They may also show irritability and general dissatisfaction. Nothing pleases them. Such children may "bug you" a lot because the tired child has no energy to self-entertain.

Unfortunately children do not come with a built-in system for self-regulation of sleep. They know when they are hungry or thirsty but they don't always know when they are tired. From a survival point of view, it's probably more important to let an adult know you are hungry or thirsty than tired.

Perhaps the main reason children don't always know they are tired is that there are so many stimuli in the world to keep them awake, including such things as electric lights. For millennia children did not need to know whether they were tired or not; when it got dark, everybody went to sleep.

I no longer think it's mandatory to have an early bedtime, because so many parents both work. They want and need time with their baby when they get home.

But I do think it's important that: **1)** Babies and children get enough sleep. **2)** Parents learn to read their child's I-need-more-sleep signals. **3)** Parents gently help train their child to an earlier bedtime when school starts.

Siblings

ParenTips:

- *Repeat after Me: Sibling Rivalry Is Not a Disease! No Treatment Is Necessary. Children LEARN From Sibling Squabbling.*

- *Prepare an Older Child for a Coming Baby. Tell the Facts and Talk About FEELINGS.*

- *Interfere Only When Person or Property in Jeopardy.*

- *Spend Time with EACH CHILD ALONE.*

- *Don't Obsess Over Fairness—Treat Each Child According to His or Her UNIQUE NEEDS.*

When parents ask me, "What should I do about sibling rivalry?" I tell them that it doesn't require treatment, it's not a disease. But you can learn how to minimize sibling squabbling and make your house more peaceful.

Sibling squabbling can drive parents up the wall. Most of us hate listening to children fight and argue. We weary of serving as referee between children (each of whom is convinced we favor the other). We dislike being reminded of the fights we had with our own siblings.

Perhaps what bothers parents most is reliving their own childhood and once more experiencing the painful feelings of remembered slights and perceived unfairness. Many of us carry unresolved feelings about our own siblings all our lives.

Why Do Kids Fight?

We have to ask why siblings fight in order to understand the basis of sibling rivalry. Bickering and jockeying for position seems to be a natural part of living in a family that has more than one child.

There seems to be a biological basis for such behavior. Each baby bird tries to cheep the loudest to get the worm. Growling puppies pretend to bite, practicing skills that will be needed later for defense. Squabbling is the way human siblings learn how to get along with other people and become social beings.

Squabbling siblings are learning how to deal with people their own age, give in, negotiate, express emotional feelings, accommodate the wishes of others, cope with feelings of jealously, figure out how far they can go with physical aggression, be angry with someone they love, compromise, and—if all else fails—coexist. These are valuable lessons, so valuable that parents with only one child must provide playmates and play situations so that an only child can learn them.

What can parents do to minimize the battleground atmosphere?

- *Alternate play-together with play-alone time* so children learn how to amuse themselves.

- Have suggestions about things children can do when they seem bored with playing. I'm convinced that a good deal of the fighting between sibs results from boredom. Picking a fight sparks things up a bit.

- *Forbid destructive behavior against people or property.* Tussling is OK; hitting with a baseball bat is not. Also, siblings cannot be permitted to destroy each other's possessions.

- If the noise or the unpleasantness is getting to you, even if neither child nor property is at risk, you have every right to *separate the children.* Interpret your actions for them by saying it's not pleasant to be near bickering people. It's a good idea to have solitary activities for each child in mind so you know how to handle the inevitable "There's nothing to do!" lament.

- *Assign blame as sparingly as possible.* Sometimes a child is out of line and needs to be dealt with. However the best thing a parent can do is let children resolve their own disputes. Listen to what each child says is the problem but don't come up with the solution yourself. Rather, rephrase the problem as you heard it ("Jeff wants to study and Nancy is playing her stereo too loud. How can you kids settle this? It's been a problem ever since Nancy got her new stereo."). Remember if you tell the kids how to settle it, you create a winner and a loser. If they settle things themselves it's a negotiated settlement.

Equal and Fair: An Impossible Goal

Many parents tell me that their children accuse them of unequal and unfair treatment. They describe each child as insatiable when it comes to parental time or attention.

When I was bringing up my children I worried much too much about my own childhood feelings toward my own sibling. I spent many years trying to be scrupulously fair to each of my children because I thought that my parents weren't fair to me (I now know that my sister thought I was the one who got the most attention!).

Because I was determined always to be fair and treat my children equally, I made a conscious decision to be the fairest parent ever. If I bought something for one child, I felt compelled to buy something for the other. I even got the non-birthday child a non-birthday present on the sibling's birthday!

Such a misguided notion of equality is not only impossible to achieve; it isn't even desirable. How much more loving it is to treat each child according to his or her own needs and wishes! How foolish to assume each wants what the other does! Now I know that when children are whining for equality or fairness, they don't want it, they want to be **special.**

Let's face it. The world is not fair. And parents cannot make it so. As a matter of fact—although I did not know this when my own children were small—parents can make things worse by trying to treat one child in exactly the same way as another. The goal is not to treat your children equally, but **uniquely.**

The best way to show children that we love them is to stop worrying about treating them equally and start treating them according to their individual needs. This means **seeing them as individuals and being attentive to their individual needs and wants.**

There are several parenting books on the market that I wish had been available when I needed them. *Siblings Without Rivalry* by Adele Faber and Elaine Mazlish is one of them.

The authors point out in a chapter called, "Equal Is Less" that parents bring on a lot of sibling difficulties. When we emphasize fairness and equality, we de-emphasize uniqueness. We ourselves may make each child think that mother never gives enough, because mother herself is always worrying about how to be fair.

None of us will ever have enough time or money or attention for a child who feels we are not being fair. Such a child can seem insatiable because he or she does not feel special. "To be loved equally is somehow to be loved less. To be loved uniquely—for one's own special self—is to be loved as much as we need to be loved."

So the wise parent will **give according to need** ("Do you want a few grapes or a big bunch?") instead of counting out equal numbers of grapes. The same concept applies to time spent with each child ("I know I'm spending a lot of time going over your sister's composition. It's important to her. As soon as I'm finished, I want to hear what's important to you.").

When you stop to think about it, every one of us needs to be loved not because of our attributes, achievements, or behaviors but just for being ourself.

In a similar vein, each of us deserves to be loved because of being oneself—not because we are somebody's brother or sister. We should each get what we need, not get what a fairness-freak thinks we should get!

Dr. Heins' Guidelines for Raising Siblings

The Heins twelve guidelines for harmonious sibling relationships follow:

- *Prepare* the older child for the birth of the new baby. Give the child an opportunity to think about feelings as well as facts. ("How will you feel when Mommy is busy taking care of the new baby? "How will you feel when the new baby takes away your toy?")

- *Love each child for his or her wonderful uniqueness.* Make sure each child knows he or she is special and unique.

- Treat each child uniquely and *forget about the unattainable quest for equality.*

- *Spend time with each child separately.* As a busy mother I remember how convenient it was to lump my own two together as "the children." But **every**

child needs some special, focused time alone with each parent every day. (SEE PAGE 183)

- Be sure each child has exclusive use of some space. Even if the children share a room, see to it that each child has some *space* to call "my own" as well as some personal toys.

- *Do not compare* children—either unfavorably or favorably.

- *Do not assign a role* to a child ("He's the pushy one.")

- *Expect squabbling* among siblings. Sibling rivalry can be minimized but never eliminated. Squabbling helps siblings learn how to live with others.

- *Ignore* sibling squabbling whenever possible. Step in only: **1)** to stop any hurtful action against a child or the child's property or **2)** if the noise level gets unbearable.

- *Allow each child to express his or her feelings,* even negative feelings, about a sibling. Help the child identify the feeling ("You sound angry!") and teach the child how to express feelings without hurting the other person. "I am angry at you because you tore my Star Wars poster!" is acceptable. "You're a clumsy retard who is too dumb to tape something to a wall!" is not.

- *Think about yourself and your own siblings.* I have three "**R**" suggestions for adult siblings: **R**emember, **R**ecount (tell your children about how you felt), and **R**esolve any unresolved issues.

- *Talk about yourself and your own siblings.* How did you resolve spats? How did you deal with strong feelings? While children are trying to grow up they sometimes feel as though they'll never get there. Listening to parents share their own stories can provide more than information about an incident. It also points out that all grown-ups were once children, which is sort of encouraging!

- Model ways of expressing feelings without hurting the other person by using I-statements and avoiding put-downs. Show your children affection and tolerance between their parents. They will learn from this how to become affectionate and tolerant toward their siblings.

Siblings Who Are Very Different

What about family dynamics when one child is unquestionably brighter or more talented than another? Should parents be concerned about one child's developing a complex and growing up in the shadow of the gifted sibling?

As I have already said, all siblings in all families should be treated by their parents *uniquely* not *equally*. This means loving each child as an individual and, furthermore, means developing understanding and insight about each child. We gain insight by spending time alone with each child and listening to that child in such a way that we really hear what is being said and perceive what the child is really feeling.

Here are some suggestions:

- Don't expect the gifted and not-gifted child to be comparable as far as the amount of effort each child puts into school work. By definition, school is a breeze for the gifted child which is the reason it's so important to find that child other challenges at school and at home.

- Don't expect the average child to do as well as the gifted one. Instead expect each child to do the best he or she can.

- Do some intensive *"niche-picking."* Help the non-gifted child find areas based on his or her own interests and abilities which do not compete with those of the gifted child.

- *Praise children specifically.* Global praise like, "What a smart girl you are!" may be looked on with suspicion by the child who knows he or she does not have the sibling's abilities and gifts. Use phrases like, "Getting a B+ in English took real effort. You can be proud of yourself!"

- Separate children academically by sending them to different schools if possible.

- Separate their outside activities too. If both like sports perhaps you can steer one toward tennis, the other toward swimming. If they are musical, guide one to the violin, the other to the flute. Better to compete with peers and self rather than each other.

- When the time comes for a special reward, find appropriate ones for each child. Take them to different events sometimes and be sure to spend time alone with each child.

- Don't let your own feelings about competition or struggling to keep up with a sibling take over. Perhaps you worry more about these matters than the child does.

- Trust your non-gifted child to deal with this reality of his or her life. Don't expect the child to "develop a complex." The child may instead develop a realistic understanding of life, a deep understanding of his or her own strengths, and a loving respect for the sibling's accomplishments.

Over twenty years ago in *Your Child's Self-Esteem,* Dorothy Corkville Briggs (Dolphin Books, 1975) reminded parents that they are mirrors which their children use to build their psychological identity. A child who knows that he or she is **1)** lovable (i.e., is loved for being his or her unique self, not just accomplishments) and **2)** worthwhile (i.e. is competent and this competence is recognized) will have self-esteem. And such a child will have the necessary psychological "armor" to live his or her life without negative emotions like sibling envy.

Parents can mirror for each child a loving reflection of the child's unique self and worth.

I like to think that, after a generation of children is brought up by parents who understand the difference between treating children equally and treating them uniquely, there will be fewer adults still smarting over perceived parental unfairness. Who knows? This could lead to a more pleasant and more peaceful world.

Self-Esteem

- *Repeat after Me: You Can't Give Self-Esteem like a Present.*

- *Love Each Child for His or Her Own Sake.*

- *Foster Self-Calming.*

- *Encourage Competencies.*

- *Praise Specifically.*

Self-esteem is sweeping the country. Parents and teachers worry constantly, "Am I providing the child with self-esteem?"

Alas, this approach is all wrong. You can't give self-esteem like a present, all wrapped up with a pretty bow!

How DO parents raise children with self-esteem?

Self-esteem is grounded on and supported by two "pillars." Visualize a bridge held up by two pillars, both of which are essential. The first pillar is **unconditional love** which enables the child to learn self-love. The second pillar is **competency** which gives the child the inner strength that comes from knowing, "I can do it by myself!"

Parents today are attuned to the meaning of unconditional love—loving the child for his or her unique self, not attributes or accomplishments or appearance. Parents also understand that they should meet an infant's needs so the baby will develop a sense of trust and an understanding that the world is a pretty good place. When you're hungry or wet, a nice big person comes and feeds and changes you.

Parents are not all attuned to the concept of self-calming, however. Fearful they will harm the child's sense of trust and positive world view, parents hesitate to let their baby cry.

All of us struggle with ambiguity. And here is a great big ambiguity in terms of advice given to parents. When the baby is little, parents should strive to meet every need promptly. When the baby is older—three months or so—parents should give the baby increasing time to self-calm. Parents should now allow babies to cry a bit and learn to comfort themselves. This is the first **competency.**

The next set of capabilities come with crawling and toddling. Wise parents childproof a child's environment not only to allow but also to encourage **safe exploration.** Still later comes rough-and-tumble-play, climbing on slides, etc. With every accomplishment the pillar grows higher. **"I can do it myself!"**

Later come the competencies of **responsibility** and **learning.** Start chores early; even toddlers can put toys away and carry a cup to the sink. And, of course, encourage a love of learning and let your child know you expect a good perform-ance at school.

Beware of global, continuous praise. "What a good girl you are!" When chil-dren hear this phrase over and over it becomes meaningless, they tune it out. Furthermore, children are realists; they know they are not always good so a credi-bility gap creeps in. Finally, if you put your child on a pedestal the poor kid has no place to go but down!

Toilet Topics:
Basic Training, Bed-Wetting

ParenTips:

BASIC TOILET-TRAINING

- *Start Toilet Training When Child Is Ready:*
  Has an interest in what people do in the toilet.
  Can walk and run.
  Can sit quietly.
  Can understand simple requests.
  Can communicate needs.

- *Use the Heins Method:*
  Prepare.
  Place.
  Praise (but don't pressure).

- *Involve Child Care Workers in Training.*

- *Investigate Medically If There Is a Significant Delay.*

BED-WETTING

- *Need Do Nothing If Bed-Wetter Is Under Five.*

- *After Age Five:*
  Conditioning alarm.
  Medication.
  Do nothing.

- *Child Owns Problem.*
  Towel on bed.
  Child takes towel and wet PJs to washer.

Toilet Training

Toilet training should start **when the child is ready** for it. By eighteen months maturation of the nerves which control the process of defecation has occurred, so most pediatricians advise parents not to start toilet training until then.

How can you tell whether YOUR child is ready to be trained?

- The child demonstrates an interest in the toilet and what people do there.

- The child has an awareness of being wet or soiled—or, better yet, an awareness that soiling is about to happen.

- The child has mastered walking and running. The ability to walk and run means the ability to start and stop an activity.

- The child can sit and play quietly for at least a few minutes at a time.

- The child can understand simple requests.

- The child can communicate his or her needs.

At about eighteen months of age evaluate your child against this checklist. If a child can do these things, then he or she is ready and it's time to start the training process. In my own experience, I have found most children are not ready until they are close to their second birthday.

Children develop according to their own timetables, which means a few may be ready before eighteen months and some will not be ready until they are over two.

Technology has brought us furnaces, washing machines, and disposables. No harm will come to two-year-olds still in diapers—and mothers are no longer slaves to diaper-boiling.

Bowel and daytime bladder control will occur at about two-and-a-half to three in normal children, whether or not training was started at nine months or two years. Starting early does not mean you will finish early. Rather it means you will spend a **longer** time in the process of training.

Today's mothers, especially those who work outside the home, are very busy so I try to give advice that will make things as easy for them as possible. My advice about training is to wait because the later you start, the less time you will have to spend on the task.

There is also a child-centered reason to delay toilet training. If you wait until the child is old enough to be truly involved in the process, you can use the process of toilet training to help the child **achieve autonomy.** A child who can pull down his or her own pants to go to the toilet has become quite independent.

*I recommend my **Prepare, Place,** and **Praise** (but no pressure) method.*

1) *Prepare* the child by letting the child see what the parents and older children do with their stool and urine. It's a good idea to let a toddler accompany the parent to the toilet so the child can observe the whole sequence from taking off the pants to wiping and flushing. Don't just sit there, tell the child what you are doing and why you are doing it where you are doing it. Show the child what you have "made." Let the child watch you flush and later flush for you (if the noise and disappearance frightens your child, back off and wait a while before asking the child to flush again).

When you are changing the child's diaper, show and tell your child what he or she made. Tell the child it is the same product that you made and it goes in the same place.

2) *Place* the fully-clothed child on the potty to practice sitting there. I recommend a child-sized potty chair on which the child can sit without your help rather than the type of potty which fits on the toilet. When you think the child is ready to have a bowel movement, place him or her, fully clothed, on the potty. When he or she performs, let the child help you put the stool from the diaper into the potty. After a couple of weeks, place the unclothed child on the potty and wait for the desired results.

3) *Praise*—and reward with a small goody—the child's performance. Stress that the child is doing what grown-ups do and that you are pleased. But don't pressure the child. If you aren't getting anywhere, or if the child balks at any step of the process, back off for a bit and start all over again later.

Few mothers working outside the home today are able to arrange a leave of absence for toilet training. I myself trained two children while working full time, so I know it can be done.

Talk with your child's caretaker about your philosophy and approach. Involve this person in the decision about when the child is ready. Communicate frequently about the child's progress. Tell each other about any balking or problems.

Remember the child has a lot to learn about using the toilet. Children must understand what adults expect them to do with their excretions. They have to realize what it feels like before they have to go, know how to get to the potty, figure out how to remove clothing quickly and sit down in time, and learn to relax the sphincter muscles to let the feces or urine out. A monumental task for a two-year-old.

So a child should be ready to learn and the parents should give the child time to learn all this stuff.

Problems with Training

When parents come to me because they have a child near to, or over, age four who is not yet toilet trained, I first prescribe a big dose of parental relaxation. I tell them they did not do anything wrong, they do not need to blame themselves or get upset when other mothers brag how easy toilet training was at their house.

There are several reasons for delayed (notice I use the word "delay" because all children with normal bodies and brains will eventually become trained) training. Sometimes parents start too early, which means they usually have to stop and start later so it takes longer. Sometimes there is an event in the child's life like the birth of a sibling, illness, or loss of a loved one that causes regression. Rarely there is an emotional problem in the child and/or the parent. Sometimes parents are not skilled in dealing with young children and a power struggle results—with the fight arena located at the toilet bowl. Also, some children are frightened by the toilet itself, which is noisy and causes objects to disappear and never be seen again.

What to Do When Your Child WON'T

If your child really balks at using the potty, I suggest you **stop.** Learning to use the toilet is a complex process. The child has to **feel** the full bladder or rectum, **control** the emptying, and **give up the freedom** to deposit body wastes when and wherever he or she pleases.

All of this learning takes time. And learning does not always proceed along a straight line. There are peaks and valleys. Or there may be a long period of refusal.

If you are dealing with a child, under four, I suggest saying, "I'm going to put the potty chair away for a while. You are getting bigger every day and pretty soon we'll try again."

How long do you wait before restarting? Wait a few weeks and then go over your readiness list again. Sometimes the child will ask you to get out the potty again. Do it! Children are very good at knowing when they are ready to do things.

If your child is four or older I suggest a different approach. Give the older child **responsibility** for the training process.

- Tell your child he or she is big enough to use the toilet like big people do.

- If the child poops in the diaper, ask the child to help you dispose of the BM and explain that grown-ups put their stool in the toilet. "You are big enough to do that even if you first put it in the diaper."

- Tell the child that every time he or she poops in the potty you will award a gold star. Have your child make a chart for the stars. After seven or ten stars the child gets a small treat. This is a reward for a "good performance" analogous to a bonus at work.

- Be sure the child knows you **want** the child to be trained but you **understand** if he or she is not yet ready. This is the time to remind yourself that you love the child even if you are annoyed at or worried about the behavior.

Encopresis

A fairly common cause of delayed training is physiological. Some children are born with a tendency to produce large stools. This causes pain and subsequent

64

reluctance to pass stool. Some children do not feel the presence of stool in the rectum, the signal of a need to defecate. This may be something the child is born with or may result from having the rectum stretched by the large stools the child is withholding in order to avoid pain.

The term **encopresis** is used when a child over the age of four regularly deposits stool in underwear or other inappropriate places. About 1 percent of second-graders have this problem. Boys are affected six times more frequently than girls. Usually the child defecates infrequently and often abdominal pain is present. School-age children may be teased by classmates which adds to the child's distress.

A child who seems reluctant to pass a stool, especially in the toilet, and goes for days without a bowel movement, very often is experiencing pain on defecation or has had pain at some time in the past. Because this could be encopresis, I recommend that such a child be seen by a pediatric gastroenterologist (or a pediatrician with a sympathetic interest in this sort of problem). The child needs a complete examination including an examination of the rectum and possibly X-rays to show how much stool is being retained.

The pediatric gastroenterologist will make the diagnosis and start treating the child. Treatment consists of **1)** education and explanation, **2)** removal of the retained stool by means of enemas or laxatives, **3)** diet and medicines to keep the stools soft to prevent pain on passage, **4)** a "new" training regimen with the child sitting on the toilet for a specified time twice a day and suitable rewards, like gold stars, for performance.

In my experience the combination of **1)** a good doctor who knows about this problem and **cares** and **2)** parents who understand the problem and comply with the regimen prescribed will conquer the problem in almost all cases. Because of the physiological basis for encopresis, there may need to be a "maintenance" regimen to keep the stools soft.

The key to this problem is to realize that the child is not doing this deliberately and the parents did not cause it.

Bed-Wetting (Enuresis)

Bed-wetting has plagued parents and children since time immemorial. As a matter of fact, a treatment for enuresis, which is defined as involuntary discharge of urine, was described in an Egyptian papyrus in 1550 BC. It probably didn't work!

What most parents of bed-wetting children worry about **is not enuresis** because it occurs in young children (although the bed is just as wet!). The term nocturnal or sleep enuresis (involuntary discharge of urine during sleep) is reserved for boys over age six and girls, who generally achieve bladder control earlier than boys, over age five. Children younger than this who wet at night are exhibiting perfectly normal behavior.

What do we know about bed-wetting in children old enough to warrant using the term? In the first place it is fairly common, affecting 5 percent of ten-year-olds and 1 percent of fifteen-year-olds. Bed-wetting is more common in boys than in girls and it runs in families. As a matter of fact, the risk that the child will be affected increases six-fold if the mother or father was a bed-wetter. Another study showed that children with a family history of bed-wetting took an average of one-and-a-half years longer to achieve nighttime bladder control than did children without such a family history.

An annoying disorder as common as enuresis is bound to lead to many folk remedies as well as many theories as to what causes it. Although once thought to be a sleep disorder with a defective arousal mechanism, recent studies have disproved this theory by showing that bed-wetting is independent of sleep stage. Some doctors postulated a defect in the size or efficacy of the bladder but this doesn't seem to be the case. And, as in the case of most behavior problems in children, there are always some experts who believe there is a psychological component—the child wets the bed to get even with the parents sort of nonsense.

The very latest research points to nighttime urine production as a cause of nocturnal enuresis. We know that the bladder has to be full for enuresis to occur. Evidently some children who wet the bed have not developed a normal nocturnal anti-diuresis mechanism. This means that, unlike the rest of us, these children do not decrease urine production at night. The amount of urine they produce at night far exceeds their daytime bladder capacity.

There are two basic approaches to the treatment of enuresis in childhood. One is to do nothing and wait for the child to outgrow it. This is effective. Any bed-wetter has about a 15 percent chance of the problem's going away during the course of a given year which means that the vast majority of children stop wetting the bed before they are in their teens. If the parents and child can tolerate the extra laundry and the stigma, it's OK to wait patiently.

In my experience, however, many children are troubled by not being able to control their bladder at night although their friends can. They are ashamed to sleep over at a friend's house. Bed-wetting children themselves interpret the symptom as evidence of being babyish. Studies have shown that measurements of children's self-concept increased after enuresis was treated. I personally think life is tough enough for kids today without having to deal with this troublesome symptom.

If parents decide to help their child get over this problem, there are two forms of treatment to consider: conditioning (behavior modification) or pharmacological (drug) treatment.

There is absolutely no evidence at all that punishment (although punishment for something the child cannot help is cruel, one-third of parents queried "treat" bed-wetting with punishment), waking the child to go to the bathroom, or withholding fluids after a certain hour do any good at all.

Conditioning therapy involves buying a urine alarm, a device that sounds a buzzer when the child first begins to void. The child gradually is conditioned to awaken when the bladder is full. This method can work. There is up to a 70 percent success rate and a low relapse rate after the treatment is stopped.

Imipramine (Tofranil) is an antidepressant drug which works in some cases of enuresis. Success rates approach 40 percent and other children improve though they are not cured. A new approach using desmopressin also looks promising. This drug acts like the antidiuretic hormone, which these children do not produce at night in increased quantities as normal children do.

My first advice to parents is not to pin the label of "bed-wetter" on any child too young to deserve it. Try simple home remedies for the young child struggling to achieve night bladder control. With my own children, I left a light on in the bathroom, dressed them in training pants or loose, easy-to-get-out of pajamas, folded a thick towel on the bed, and left another pair of pajamas and folded towel within reach. If the child had an accident it was a simple thing to change and put the wet towel in the hamper and the dry towel on the bed without waking up the parents. This helped give the child a sense of mastery over the situation.

If your child wants help with bed-wetting, start with a visit to the pediatrician to make sure there is no urinary infection or diabetes. Ideally the parents and the doctor would talk over the two types of treatment and decide together which to try first. If it were my child I'd try the urine alarm because, so far, it has the best cure rate, the lowest relapse rate, and no drug side effects. However if this didn't work, I would not hesitate to use either imipramine or desmopressin under careful medical supervision.

Be sure the child understands that he or she is going to the doctor for *help with a problem,* not because the child is bad or a baby or because the parents are at their wit's end.

Sexuality/Gender

ParenTips:

- *Sexuality Education Begins at Home—Early.*

- *Be an "Askable" Parent.*

- *Work to Get Comprehensive Sexuality Education in the Schools.*

- *Masturbation Is Universal and Harmless.*
  "We don't do that in public."

- *Playing Doctor Is Common and Harmless.*

- *Parental Nudity—You Decide but Stop Before Child Is Three.*

- *Respect Child's Privacy Needs.*

- *Convey Fact That Every Child Owns His or Her Own Body.*

- *Teach Good Touch/Bad Touch (Tell Grown-Up in Charge).*

- *Do Everything You Can to Avoid Gender-Stereotyping.*

Sexuality Education

In the past parents weren't into early sexuality education. When Junior reached puberty Dad was supposed to tell him to not get a girl in trouble or contract a disease. And Mom was supposed to talk to Sis about menstruation, prefer-ably before it happened. Both kids, of course, got lots of misinformation from their equally uninformed peers long before their parents spoke up.

The world has changed. Unless you want your young child to learn about sex from MTV you must be prepared to field early questions about sexuality your-self.

Because there is no way parents can shut out the world, they have to "inter-pret" the world for their children in terms of the family's values. Even the six o'clock news could have a story on child prostitution or teen pregnancy. Your job is to discuss what the child sees, point out "We don't do that in our family," and find ways to start a dialogue with the child.

Start early. If you don't answer the questions your child asks about sex at all, or if you answer them in a constrained way, sex stands out as a somehow dif-ferent topic. Your child's curiosity about sex may be heightened, not because you have given the child *too much information* as is often thought, but because you have turned an innocent question into an unanswerable one.

Don't worry about telling too much. Children process all information whether it's about sex or Santa Claus in the same way. They transform the infor-mation to their own level of understanding. And, of course, that level is deter-mined by the child's age. This means that children who are too young to under-stand what they hear simply do not process the material; it goes right over their heads.

The "rule" about early sexuality education is simple: **Answer Questions When They Are Asked.** And if a child reaches five or so without asking, bring the subject up yourself by talking about a friend who is having a baby, for exam-ple.

How much should you tell and how explicit should you be? The trick is to tell the child a little bit more than is necessary to answer the question.

The reason you provide somewhat more information than the child asks for is to make it very clear that you are what educator and author Sol Gordon calls "an askable parent." Your children learn that you willingly provide honest answers and you don't get embarrassed or angry or make jokes when they bring up the subject of sex. In today's world, where the media present such a blatantly inaccu-rate and glorified view of sex, it's more important than ever that a child have an askable parent.

Askable parents are the first and most important sex educators of their children. Ideally parents provide accurate information, convey the idea that sex is natural and pleasurable, and instill the sense of responsibility toward self and partner that must always must accompany this natural pleasure.

I know from the experiences I had with my own children that it can be difficult to talk to children about such an intimate matter as sex, no matter how committed one is to the concept of sex education. It took an effort on my part to overcome my hesitancy and learn how to become comfortably askable.

What does it take to become an "askable parent"?

- A commitment to sexuality education which starts at home and continues in the schools.

- A comfortable working knowledge of human sexuality.

- An understanding of sexuality in the infant and child.

- Knowledge about child development so that you know when to expect questions and how the child's mind works.

- Comfort with your own sexuality, as well as comfort with demonstrating affection in front of the children.

- The ability to communicate with your child, because sex education is much more than presenting the facts; there must also be a dialogue between parent and child in order to discuss **values.**

- Willingness to work with your child's school to ensure that your child has the opportunity to deal with this subject with professional teachers and peers in a classroom.

Masturbation

Young babies touch their bodies as soon as they can move their hands around. When they discover that touching their genitals feels good they may deliberately do it in order to experience this feeling. This does not mean the child is oversexed or depraved or will become sexually active at an early age. It merely means the child is clever enough to figure out what feels good.

When young children get older and gain more motor control they may rub themselves against the bed or crib to get pleasure. Some children rock back and forth, others thrust their pelvis against a chair or stuffed animal. Some children may get red in the face and pant as though they are having an orgasm. Many just rub until they are tired of the activity.

Parents are often upset when they see a child masturbate because it is hard for some people to accept that young children are sexual rather than innocent, especially if the parents were themselves raised to think of sex as something shameful.

Such activity is normal and harmless. Parents should be pleased that their child can enjoy his or her body without shame. However parents have a very important task in that they must teach the child about the relationship between private parts and privacy.

Tell your child that you know it feels good; everybody likes to feel good. But this part of the body is a "private part." And touching there is something people do in private. You can explain this as casually as you tell your children not to pick their noses in public.

If you find your child masturbating in private, you can say, "Excuse me." and leave. This helps get across the concept that you too want privacy at certain times.

Child psychologist Penelope Leach (1989, page 485) phrases it well: "You may gently persuade (the child) to keep this pleasure to private times, as a matter of good manners..." Because this is something we do in private, people do not want to see us do it in public.

Never tell the child this is wrong or will cause harm to the genitals. Be especially gentle when talking to little boys who may already be afraid they will "lose it" because they have seen little girls without one.

Genital Touching

Not all genital handling is masturbation, which is defined as handling the genitals so as to produce orgasm. But handling the genitals is pleasurable and children can use this pleasurable sensation to distract themselves when they feel stressed or fatigued.

They discover on their own that it feels good to rub "down there" just as it feels good to scratch an itch. (By the way, the child might just have an itch; not all touching of the genitals is sexual!)

Psychoanalytic theory holds that one reason a little boy clutches at his penis is to reassure himself that it is still there. He has been worried about losing it ever since he saw a little girl and realized not everybody has one. Later he will be able to sort people into two groups—male and female—and accept the fact that they are different. But now all he knows is: "I've got one, she doesn't, something must have taken it off, I better hold on to mine so nothing happens to it."

This fear begins sometime between the ages of two and four, just at the time a child is also extremely fearful of any kind of bodily damage. The slightest scratch necessitates a Band-Aid and a hug, while the sight of a real injury on one's self or another can be terrifying.

It is true that very young children have sexual feelings, that the preschooler has great fear of bodily mutilation, and that psychoanalytic theory has a plausible explanation for castration fears in the child. But my own personal opinion is that many young boys clutch at their penis because it is there! The length of the arms places the hands in just the right position to touch the genitals.

What should you do about genital touching? Many parents get upset when their son handles his genitals and most, even those who understand it is a harmless habit which will go away by itself, do not want other people to see this habit.

Prevention is the first line of defense. Try to keep your child as free of fatigue and stress as possible.

Consider the habit a *signal* and treat it as such. Say something like, "I see you feel tired, Tommy. Let me help you get ready for bed early and then I'll read you a story".

If it happens in public, bend down to have a private word with your son. "We don't touch ourselves there in public when there are other people around." Just a gentle reminder is all that's needed and be sure the "public" doesn't hear what you're saying. The last thing you want to do is embarrass your son in public for a harmless behavior you don't wish him to do in public.

Obviously, if a child constantly engages in genital touching, there could be a problem requiring investigation. Otherwise don't worry about it. Children learn very quickly what behaviors are acceptable in public.

Nudity

It would be great if parents could feel comfortable enough about their own bodies and their own sexuality to bathe and undress in front of their young children as though this were the most natural thing in the world—which it is.

This gives a clear message to the child that there is nothing shameful or bad about bodies. It enables children to notice that people come in two varieties and therefore Mommy and Daddy look different. It also gives the child a natural opportunity to ask time-honored questions such as, "How come you have one and I don't?" or "How come yours are bigger than mine?" And it gives the parents a natural opportunity to name body parts accurately and matter-of-factly.

However, most parents feel uncomfortable doing this and should not walk around naked indefinitely. Why? **1)** Children must learn about the importance of privacy in our culture and **2)** Parental nudity can be overly stimulating for older preschoolers.

Privacy is a very important issue and "owning one's own body" is an important lesson to teach young children. Therefore it is not a good idea to let your children touch you in any private places. Sometimes a curious child will ask, "Why can I touch your nose and not your penis?" or "How come the baby can suck your nipple and I can't?" The answers, which should be given in a very casual manner, are "This is a private place and I don't want other people to touch it unless I say so." and "When you were a baby you got milk out of my breast just like the baby does but my breasts are a private place and I don't want people to touch them unless I say so."

You can use two approaches when it comes to deciding at what age you stop appearing naked in front of your child. You can think about your own feelings. Would you feel uncomfortable if a neighbor child the same age as your child saw you naked? For most of us that age is probably somewhere between two and three. You can also think about your child's feelings and his or her developing sense of privacy. Children in the so-called Oedipal stage are "in love" with the parent of the opposite sex and parental nudity may be over-stimulating. Most preschoolers want to toilet and bathe by themselves when they are around five.

Avoid Gender Stereotyping

We all know that there are biological differences between males and females. Children learn this quite early. If you say to a girl as young as eighteen months, "What a cute boy you are!" she will laugh or shake her head. This knowledge—the basic identification of self as male or female—is called core gender identity and is firmly established before the age of three. By four the child understands that gender is permanent and can't be changed.

Children also acquire gender roles by adopting those behaviors which society says go with each gender. Children may be very sex-stereotypic during the preschool period because this is the way they learn how to be male or female. Even in a very non-sex-stereotypic home the little boy may insist only boys can be doctors. The daughter of a woman doctor may insist girls grow up to be nurses.

Gender roles are made up of culturally determined factors. Gender role stereotypes come to pass when human characteristics that either men or women can have, such as nurturing or compliance or athletic ability, are seen as biologically determined absolutes. If society believes that girls are docile and compliant and boys are tough and aggressive, these messages become embedded in our children. Not only are their childhoods constricted but they are ill-prepared for adult life in today's society.

Sexism uses gender role stereotyping but goes much further. It is based on the belief that there is a natural hierarchy and men belong at the top. Such a misguided notion damages healthy personality development in both girls and boys. Girls may feel they should not be assertive because it is not expected of them. Boys grow up afraid to express feelings, which in turn unduly pressures men and affects their relationships with women.

OK, sexist child rearing is bad. Now what can parents specifically do to help their daughters become assertive and their sons become nurturing?

● Avoid sex-role stereotyping in your household. Be especially careful about the chores assigned. Ask both boys and girls to set the table and do yard work.

● Raise every girl with the expectation she will be able to support herself and raise every boy with the expectation that he will be able to do all household chores.

● Interpret what the child sees on TV. Point out that men as well as women can wash the kitchen floor and that women can be astronauts and astrophysicists.

● Make sure there are role models in every daughter's life so she can see for herself that women can be doctors and men can be nurses.

● Be vigilant about degrading or derogatory remarks made about women. If you can't stop your daughter from hearing such put-downs, at least point out how awful they are.

- Encourage daughters to be more concerned about who they are and what they know and think than they are about how they look.

- Find books for your children that dispel some of the destructive myths which abound in sexism like men don't cry or women don't become governors.

- Encourage your daughters to have personal courage. Gender-linked timidity (feeling and acting timid because it is expected of girls) is a barrier to women.

- Give your sons permission to have tenderness and sensitivity.

- Monitor what your children are picking up at school. Don't let them grow up thinking math is for boys and dancing is for girls.

Bothersome Stages

Biting

Hitting

Head-Banging

Clinging to a Baby Blanket

Clinging to Parents

Sharing

Whining

Negativity/Oppositional Behavior

Talking Back

Temper Tantrums

Swearing/"Bathroom Talk"

Dawdling

Pouting and Sulking

Interrupting

Lying

Biting

- *Prevent If You Can.*

  Keep your fingers away from baby's mouth!

- *Whenever Biting Occurs, Take Action!*

BABY

"No! Biting hurts!"
Pick up baby immediately.
Place in crib or playpen to remove from the scene.

TODDLER

Supervise all toddler play experiences.
Appoint "Designated Toddler-Watcher."
Don't let toddler be overwhelmed by other children.
If biting occurs, immediately remove child from play.

- *ALWAYS Remove the Biter from the Situation AND from Your Attention.*

- *Must Do This Every Time to Extinguish Biting Behavior.*

Biting in babies and toddlers is both common and normal behavior but there is a different underlying cause in each age group.

Babies Who Bite

In babies under a year, biting is an extension of mouthing behavior. Everything goes into the mouth and everything gets sucked and chewed. This chewing behavior accelerates when the baby is teething. So one day the baby's teeth clamp down on Mother's hand or face.

Such biting does not seem to be aggressive. Rather it seems to be exploratory—"I wonder what would happen if I closed my teeth when Mother's finger is in my mouth?" Of course the baby doesn't have the words to ask itself such a question but the baby can and will explore new patterns of behavior as far as possible.

Obviously the first line of defense is to keep your body parts out of the baby's mouth. But sometimes the baby will get its teeth around your cheek or shoulder before you realize what's happening.

So what should you do when your baby bites?

Say—quite sharply—"No! Biting hurts!"

If the biting persists, pick up the baby using what I call the "attention-less hold," which means you hold the baby's face away from you. You pay no more attention to the baby than you would to a sack of potatoes you carry.

Immediately transport the baby to the crib or playpen and say, "No! Biting hurts!" when you put the baby down. Repeat this *every single time* the baby bites.

In most babies biting ends because two things happen: the baby gets over teething and the baby learns that parents do not like to be bitten. Plus, you get put in a boring place if you bite.

Toddlers Who Bite

Biting behavior in the toddler and preschooler is also pretty common. Now, however, it becomes apparent that the child is exhibiting aggressive behavior.

Biting (or sometimes spitting) is usually the first aggressive behavior a child demonstrates. Shoving, hitting, or kicking comes later, when the child is better coordinated! Human development proceeds this way, starting at the head and moving out to the limbs.

Whether exploratory or aggressive, biting is **never permissible.**

How should parents handle aggressive biting? First the don'ts:

- Don't bite back.

- Don't hold the child's chin so that the child bites its own tongue.

- Don't spank.

- Don't yell at the child.

I never condone any parental behavior that deliberately causes pain to the child, especially when it is done by a parent in the name of discipline. This is demeaning and destructive parental behavior. You want the biting to stop but you also want the child to know that loving adults do not hurt children. They find other ways to stop a child's undesirable behavior.

There are several things parents of a biter *can* do:

Prevent the behavior. Biting often occurs when the young child is tired, hungry, or overwhelmed by the presence of other children.

Keep early episodes of exposure to other children **brief and simple.** Play groups should consist of only one to three same-age children.

All play experiences must be **supervised.** An adult should be right there on-site to notice signs of an impending explosion in order to "break it up." The about-to-be-biter often calms down when placed in a comforting lap or encouraged to play alone.

It won't work to put three or four toddlers together to play while the parents visit together, even when both groups are in the same room. One parent should serve in rotation as the **"Designated Toddler Watcher"** so behaviors like biting can be prevented or handled promptly. (And it follows that there should be a sufficient number of workers in childcare settings to prevent or handle aggressive acts.)

Some parents and childcare workers tell me they can see a look in a child's eye that means "I'm about to take a big bite out of someone!" What they are seeing is anger/aggression and intent to strike out. When you realize that a child is about to lose it, step in quickly!

Whenever a child bites another child, *immediately remove* the biter from the play situation. "No! Biting hurts!" are the words you use while you literally swoop up the young offender in order to isolate the biter from the other children.

Because biting is most common at an age before time-out can be an effective disciplinary tool, keep the biter on your lap or in a chair with one hand on the child's shoulder. In either case do not pay attention to the child. You do not want the youngster to get the idea that a bite leads to parental attention. Restrain the child but in an *attention-less manner,* with your head facing the opposite direction from the child's.

Every time the child bites, remove the child from the group. You will have to do this many times in the case of some young children who do not yet know how to channel their anger.

Teach the young child that *feelings have a name.* "You are angry! Let's march around the room together until the angry feelings go away!" Later you can add to the child's repertoire by showing the child how to pound a pillow or bang a drum.

Even if you are dealing with a pre-verbal child, tell the child that *everybody gets angry* and that *you understand* how it feels. But *biting is not allowed.*

Hitting

- *Unfortunately, Aggression Is Universal.*

- *Prevent Problems:*
  Avoid fatigue, hunger.
  Keep number of playmates low
  Use *Designated Toddler Watcher* at all gatherings.
  Learn to read your child's signals.

- *Never Permit Hitting.*
  Remove toddler from group at once.
  Use time-out for older children.

- *Do Not Model Aggressive Behavior.*

- *Teach Child How to Deal with Anger.*

Parents are often very upset when they see aggressive behavior in their young child. They find it hard to believe that their sweet, cuddly baby could ever do anything as mean and nasty as hitting another child over the head with a toy truck.

All children have aggressive impulses. Every human being experiences anger and exhibits aggression. Anger and aggression result from frustration, and none of us is exempt from frustration. Everyone has to learn how to handle frustration and develop self-control. But a toddler is at the very beginning of the long journey to self-control.

Aggressive behavior is so much a part of early social development in the toddler and preschooler that we wonder whether there is something wrong with the child who doesn't exhibit any.

There is a developmental sequence to aggressive behaviors in young children. When confronted with a frustration like being told "No!", the infant may cry or look bewildered or turn away, all of which are passive responses.

Passivity soon gives way to active physical aggression or strong resistance as the child becomes more adept at using arms and legs and develops a deeper sense of self that does NOT like to be thwarted. The toddler may strike the parent who sets limits, throw down the toy which is the source of frustration, or pull the hair of a non-cooperative playmate.

We don't like to see a toddler strike out, but physical aggression as a response to frustration is a necessary stage in the child's development. It means the toddler is developing an autonomous self.

The first evidence of an active response to frustration may be a temper tantrum. The kicking and screaming that go on in a tantrum are certainly active! Toddlers may throw themselves on the floor in a rage or throw the disputed toy on the floor when frustrated by a playmate. It takes a while before the child becomes "mature" enough to hit the other child. And it will be a long time before the child will use words to express aggression and to resolve conflict.

Two factors will help lessen hitting and other aggressive behaviors. First, children develop language and they gradually learn to use words instead of fists. Second, young children want to identify with and please their parents, so they gradually adopt their parents' rules of behavior.

OK, now that we know why the toddler is aggressive what do we do about it? Here are the Heins suggestions for minimizing toddler aggression:

- **Supervise all toddlers at play.** Toddlers cannot play by themselves. An adult must be close enough to swoop in and separate children when interception is indicated. If there are several children and parents in the house, be sure to pick a "Designated Toddler Watcher," someone who stays close enough to the toddlers to deal with any trouble.

- **Prevent trouble whenever possible.** Toddlers have neither a long attention span nor any mechanism for talking about their feelings. After a short time of parallel play, sit the children down to hear a story or offer a snack.

- *Learn to read your child's signals.* A good preschool teacher can intuit when there is going to be trouble. Jason gets a certain gleam in his eye or Lucy frowns just before she explodes.

- *Prevent fatigue and/or hunger.* Both of these states increase the likelihood of frustration.

- *Do not permit hitting!* The parents role is simple. Swiftly scoop the toddler up and say, "No hitting! The rule is no hitting!" You will have to repeat this many times before the child realizes that every time he or she hits the game is over. The child is in the parent's arms, no longer playing on the floor.

- *Use the "Effective Command."* (SEE PAGE 30). Speak quietly but very firmly, do not say please, because "No hitting!" is a command not a request. Always remember to say what you have to say only when you are in contact with the child. Yelling from across the room won't work.

- *Do not give explanations!* Of course *it isn't nice to hit* and *we are supposed to be gentle* and *other children don't like being hit.* But a toddler is not old enough to be reasoned with. The child does not yet have the cognitive powers to listen to reason.

- However parents should always find a way to **get in the necessary propaganda.** After you say, "No hitting!" and remove the child from the fight arena be sure to say that hitting hurts and nobody likes to get hurt. But don't start with this. You're wasting your breath and you're missing an opportunity to swoop down and remove the child from the ring instantly while the behavior is still going on.

- *Draw attention to aggressive behavior like hitting every time it happens* by taking the child away from the other children. Although this is normal behavior and we understand where it comes from, never ignore or tolerate hitting.

- Don't model aggressive behavior yourself. This means don't spank, yank, or yell.

- Teach your toddler how to deal with anger by showing the child **physical** release strategies like pounding a pillow or marching around the room and by giving the child **cognitive** assistance in figuring out feelings. This process starts when you **give the child's feelings a name.** "You are angry because Jenny took your toy. I understand, but hitting is not allowed."

- Help the child learn socially-acceptable ways to handle anger and negotiate differences. Children have to be **taught** to share or take turns.

- Don't forget it takes time for a child to learn the rules.

There are no instant results in child discipline. It takes a long time to socialize a child and a parent may have to use these strategies repeatedly many times before the child modifies his or her behavior.

Also, parents don't always use disciplinary measures in a consistent fashion. Just as aggression is a normal part of childhood behavior, inconsistency is a normal part of parental behavior. We are human and sometimes a child's behavior bugs us more than at other times. However, when dealing with aggressive behavior like hitting, parents should **strive for consistency** and patiently await results.

Head-Banging/ Body-Rocking

- *Recognize That Head-Banging Is Harmless Self-Stimulation.*

- *Pad the Crib.*

- *Ignore the Behavior and Wait for the Child to Outgrow It.*

Head-banging is fairly common and almost always completely harmless. It occurs in as many as 10 percent of young children and boys are three times more likely than girls to bang their heads. The head-banging usually starts around six or eight months and stops by age two or three.

Head-banging is one of three repetitive, rhythmic behaviors seen in young children. The others are body-rocking—the baby gets up on the hands and knees and rocks back and forth—and head-rolling—the baby rolls the head back and forth.

Head-banging is most likely to occur when the child is tired or at bedtime, when the child is upset or irritable, or when the child is alone in the crib or playpen. The behavior usually lasts less than fifteen minutes, although it may recur several times a day.

Because repetitive, rocking motions are common in autistic, blind, deaf, or retarded children, parents and doctors sometimes worry about such behaviors. But it is safe to say that head-banging children with no other symptoms of abnormality such as slow development are engaging in a harmless behavior which they will outgrow.

There is some evidence that stimulation of the inner ear that occurs when we rock back and forth may promote motor development. Also some studies have shown that children who engage in rocking behaviors are highly responsive to music.

Why Rock?

Why should normal children engage in these rhythmic behaviors? Because they enjoy it! Virtually everybody likes a rocking motion. Being in a swing or hammock or rocking chair is soothing and pleasurable.

Babies who learn how to rock for enjoyment—to self-stimulate—have a built-in mechanism for relieving tension. Do babies have tension? Of course they do. Babies are stressed by teething, by illness, by being completely dependent on someone else for everything, by being put in the crib when they still want to play, etc.

Life is great when Mommy rocks you but she isn't always around. Self-stimulation is a good substitute for Mommy as well as a rehearsal for those days ahead when she isn't around.

Pad the crib! Head-banging behavior can be quite noisy. The children may bang or rock so exuberantly that the crib moves along the floor and even hits the wall. And no parent wants to hear the sound of their child's head hitting the crib!

However hard the child seems to bang the head, head injury does not occur. Yet, understandably, most parents will both pad the crib headboard and try to anchor the crib. If the noise persists, parents can put the child's mattress on the floor. Be sure to child-proof the room and put a gate across the door lest your baby start crawling all over the house while you are asleep.

After you've taken care of the noise-abatement, **ignore the behavior and wait for it to go away!** when your child outgrows it.

My husband tells me that one of my stepsons was a head-banger who made so much noise that his crib mattress had to be placed on the floor. My daughter was a rocker who used to sing "uhh-uhh" to herself while rocking on her hands and knees. The crib creaked a lot and moved a bit but carpeting underneath kept the noise and movement down. My son neither body-rocked nor head-banged. Today my daughter is a psychiatrist and my son is a musician. Go figure.

Clinging to a Baby Blanket

ParenTips:

- *Understand Why Your Child Does This.*

- *Accept the Behavior as Normal.*

- *Ignore the Behavior.*

- *Wait for the Child to Give It Up.*

It's amazing how upset parents can get when their child clings to a babyish behavior. I think what upsets these parents is the nagging thought, "If my child doesn't give up the behavior pretty soon everybody will think the child is acting babyish or strange *and* everybody will think I'm an unskilled parent."

Why would a toddler want to go through life holding on to a ratty-looking baby blanket or a particular stuffed animal?

A child this age is going through a very important period of separation of self from mother. During this period of "transition" to selfhood, the child often seeks comfort from a familiar, soft object. Hence the term "transitional object" is given to the blanket that Linus carries around in the Peanuts comic strip. The term "treasured object" is also used.

Not all toddlers carry a security blanket around with them. Some only want the special blanket or toy at bedtime. But half of all young children do have a special attachment to an object, so this is a very common behavior.

I do not recommend taking such an object away from the child. I would be very much against sneaking it away during sleep or making up a story that some magical creature took it away. Look at it this way. If grown-ups had such harmless ways of relieving tension and anxieties, the world would be a better and safer place to live in! No drugs! No drunken drivers!

There is no reason for parents to fear their child will not be able to give up this outlet when he or she is ready. The child simply won't need it any more. Or will avoid teasing from peers by deciding that peer acceptance takes priority over an old feeling of comfort.

So one day the child will quietly leave the blanket home. Or the child may say, "I'm going to put the blanket in my closet". Many children want to know the object is available if they need it, but they no longer need to carry it around.

There is absolutely no reason to worry that a child who carries around a treasured object is excessively babyish. Of course these children are babyish. They're still babies! Children grow up soon enough; let them enjoy babyhood while they can.

There's a paradox here. Parents who are the most upset by "babyish" behavior and want their child to give up babyish ways may actually cause their child to experience anxiety, which makes the child *less likely* to give up the behavior. Parents who understand their child's needs, realize children grow out of childish needs at different rates, and make no fuss at all are likely to have children who are less anxious and more willing to give up a treasured object.

There are basic principles to deal with child behaviors like clinging to a treasured object. **1)** Understand why the child is doing it. **2)** Accept the behavior as a normal part of your developing child. **3)** Ignore the behavior; don't make a fuss over it; don't be embarrassed by it; **4)** Wait for the child to give up the behavior realizing that each child develops and matures at his or her own pace.

Clinging To Parents

- *Expect Some Clinging—All Babies Need "Emotional Refueling" as They Learn to Become Independent of Mother.*

- *You Can Minimize Clinging By:*
  Peek-a-boo Games.
  "Practice Separations."
  No Surprises!

- *When Siblings Cling, Teach Them to Take Turns by Using a Timer.*

Clinging to the parent is likely to occur in children between the ages of one and three. Clinging predictably will occur at certain times, such as when you want to leave the child with someone else at home or in preschool. Or you are busy doing something and the child wants your full attention. Or you come home from work and the child seems insatiably in need of your full attention.

Parents are often upset by clinging or demanding behavior in a young child because they think it heralds a lifetime of such behavior. It does not.

Young children are struggling to achieve autonomy and to give up what has been total dependence on the parent. But this process takes time.

When babies first begin to crawl and toddle around, they may go far away from you but will look back frequently to make sure you are still there. Or the baby will move off willingly but then return to be close to the parent for a bit. This has been described as "emotional refueling." The baby feels independent enough to move away but then becomes concerned about the distance from mother and scoots right back.

As a matter of fact, if the child and mother are in a room together and the mother moves, *even if she moves in the direction of the child,* the baby may become upset and come right to the mother. This tells us that the baby feels it is important to have the mother "anchored" in one place. Only then does the young baby feel secure.

When children grow older, other dynamics come into play. Children are no longer concerned about keeping mother in sight. They know that Mommy comes back. Now they want to *control* Mommy. The child is beginning to realize you are a separate person with your own life and interests apart from the child. Obviously the child isn't too happy about this state of affairs: "I want to control you and make you pay attention to **me!**"

Fortunately this stage doesn't last too long because the children are gaining new interests of their own every day.

It may seem paradoxical but the more secure babies feel, the less they need to cling. So one solution to clinging, crying behavior is to help the child feel secure.

Give the child lots of focused attention (SEE PAGE 183) when you can. This means you are close to the child (close enough to touch), you look at and talk to the child, and you are concentrating on activities that you and the child can do together at the child's developmental level. For example you might get down on the floor and play blocks together.

Some clinging behavior can be prevented, but nearly every child will exhibit some. Prevention efforts include playing peek-a-boo so the child happily learns Mommy disappears **and comes back**. Be sure to provide "practice separations" like leaving the child with a sitter periodically.

No surprises. Never pretend you aren't really leaving either at home or at pre-school. Always make a big thing out of saying **"Good-bye!"** and **coming back.** Praise the child for being big enough to play without you.

Tell the child where you are going and what you will be doing. Tell the child what he or she will be doing while you are gone. "Mrs Franklin will play blocks with you and make your lunch. I'll be home after lunch."

Often when a parent comes home from work, young children are demanding and clinging. It's easy to understand why—they missed you!

"Reentry" after you have been away all day is almost always a problem because **everybody has needs.** The **children** want some focused parental attention. The **parents** are tired and need to unwind and shift gears. The **family** needs supper and the house may need some attention.

The easiest way to go: **reconnect** with the children first. This can be very brief but should consist of really **focused attention** on each child. Even if a hug, "I'm so glad to see you, Sara!" and "I missed you!" is all you may have time for, **each child** needs this.

Then take a few minutes to shift gears—I always changed clothes.

If your children are clinging, set the timer and tell them you will be with them in ___ minutes. Involve the children in your relaxation sessions or cooking. Have special books or games to produce when you need to be busy.

If siblings are clinging because **each child wants you right now** try using a timer. "I'll play with Jeremy until the timer goes off and then I'll listen to Hannah tell me about school." Alternate who goes first because this can be a big issue with squabbling siblings.

Sharing

- **Teach Baby How to Feed You Tidbits and Take Food from You.**

- **Play Give-and-Take-Games like Rolling a Ball.**

- **Say "THANK-YOU!" in Very Exaggerated Tone.**

- **Teach Toddler How to Share.**
  Show that sharing can mean *more toys not less.*
  Explain how give-and-take works.

- **Talk About the Value of Sharing ("Sharing Propaganda").**

- **Prevent Problems and/or Distract Whenever You Can.**

- **Protect the Passive, Non-Aggressive Child.**

When do children learn to share willingly? Maybe never. Most of us learn to share because it's expected of us or because we are rewarded for our generous behavior. But we may never become willing sharers and greed in grown-ups abounds!

Two-year-old children are definitely not sharers. They are much more likely to engage in a behavior called "grab the toy." When they see a desirable toy, they grab it with absolutely no regard for whose toy it is. The child whose toy is grabbed is likely to hang on for dear life or use it to hit the grabber. A child this age has no sense of the advantages of sharing or taking turns.

As parents, our first impulse is to say, "Be nice! Share your toy with Josh!" Pretty futile!

There's nothing wrong with using the word "share" with a two-year-old but don't expect this command to work because your child has to be *taught what it means to share.* If you grab away your child's toy and give it to Josh, you may make your child *more* possessive—the very thing you want to prevent. Now the child thinks toys must be protected from grabbing grown-ups as well as peers.

Show young babies what sharing is. Give the baby some of your toast and ask for some in return. Make a game out of it. (Although babies may like this game, they will still go through the grabbing and squabbling stage.)

Play give-and-take games. Rolling a ball back and forth is good for starters. Then graduate to, "Bring me the red block and I'll give you the green one."

Always say, **"Thaaaannnnk you!"** in a very exaggerated tone every time the child gives you something. Your enthusiasm for what the child gives you is important.

Teach toddlers that sharing can be fun. Point out the advantages of sharing at every opportunity. Tell Jennifer that if she shares her bear with Jeremy, he will let her play with his armadillo. Explain to the children how taking turns works. "First Jimmy will play the drum and Jennifer will march. Then Jennifer will play while Jimmy marches!"

When a toy has just been grabbed, do nothing. Sometimes children as young as two will work it out—more because of their short attention span than the sudden acquisition of altruism. But stay right there so you can step in to separate the children if hostilities escalate.

Eventually both the grabber and grabbee will learn that children get something out of sharing. They get their turn, they get to play with different toys and, best of all, they win the approval of all the adults around. So keep reminding your Twos to share. Just don't expect it to happen overnight.

Try to **prevent problems** while you're waiting for your child to learn the joys of sharing by having enough sharable playthings like crayons and books. Of course both children may want the very same book at the very same moment but I never said parenting was easy. Try distraction or a small bribe. "If you give Jeremy the drum I will get you the xylophone."

Distraction is always a good ploy with preschoolers. Get all the children interested in something else or provide a toy for the one who is doing the grabbing.

There is evidence that empathy—concern for another person—can be seen very early, long before age two. But this does not conflict with the fact that two-year-olds are not willing sharers. Seeing another child crying may invoke a feeling of sympathy. But if that same child takes away a toy, look out! Generosity obviously develops later than does sympathy!

Some aggressive two-year-olds may repeatedly take toys away from another child. Don't allow such behavior. But don't panic if your child is a toy-grabber at age two. It does not mean your child will be a permanent bully.

Protect the quiet, passive, non-aggressive two-year-old. The child whose toy is grabbed may start to cry, look to you for help, or hand over the toy, not in the spirit of generosity but in a state of bewilderment. This is especially true in an only child when first exposed to other children. Try to help such a child learn to be normally assertive. "Joshua, it's your turn to play with the bear!"

Usually by the time children are three they begin to get the idea about sharing, especially if they have had plenty of opportunities to play with same-age children.

Some children in child care are very reluctant to share possessions they bring from home. Most young children in child care **like** to bring a toy from home. It reminds them of home and parents and warmth and love and security, so they do not want to give it up. Nor should they. Skilled child care workers find a way to "protect" each child's treasured objects from other children. "This blankie belongs to Max. Let's go get your Pooh-bear!"

Whining

ParenTips:

- ***Never Give In to Whining!***

- ***Be Sure Child Knows What Whining Is.***

- ***Role-Play Using "Nice Voice" and Whining Voice.***

- ***Prevent Situations That Lead to Whining.***

- ***Send Child to "Whining Place" If You Can't Take Any More.***

Every preschooler is entitled to a cranky day. The child feels out of sorts and whines. The whining merely indicates that the child is having a bad day.

However, chronic whining—the kind that drives a parent up the wall—is often unwittingly caused by the way parents react to the whining child.

How can this happen? Because parents violate a very basic rule of parenting: **Do Not Reward Bad Behavior.** To a child, all attention, including negative attention, is desirable.

Here's a common scenario in many homes: At 4:30 when the child asks for a cookie, the parent says, "Not now, you'll spoil your supper!" At 4:45 when the child whines, "I wanna cookie," the parent says sharply, "Not now, I told you!" At 4:50 the whining for a cookie starts again. This time the parent says "I can't stand your whining any more! Here's a cookie! Just be quiet!" (or shut up!—depending on how short your fuse is).

Even three-year-olds are smart enough to realize the way to get a cookie is to whine. But whether you give in, yell at the child ("Stop that whining this minute!"), or get angry and punish the child, you are providing attention. And the child, who wants attention as all children do, will continue to whine to get it. As a matter of fact the child probably wants your attention more than the cookie!

The best way to stop whining in a child is to change response behavior in the parent. When your child whines, do not give in. Be sure your child knows your firm rule. You will not give the child anything he or she asks for unless the request is made in a non-whining tone of voice.

Role-play using a normal voice and a whining voice and ask the child to do the same so you are sure the child understands what whining is and how it sounds.

If the whining continues, tell the child that whining hurts your ears. If the child can't or won't stop whining, the child will have to go to the "whining place" (somewhere out of earshot) and stay there until the whining stops. Tell the child that he or she can whine as long as it's done in the whining place where you don't have to hear it.

Be sure whiners know that they can come out of the whining place as soon as the whining stops. The child controls the length of stay by controlling the behavior. This is different from a time-out place where the child must stay until the timer goes off.

A whining place works for two reasons: **1)** The child does not get attention from the parents and **2)** The parents do not have to listen to the obnoxious sound of a whining child.

Try to prevent whining by keeping the child from getting overly tired or hungry.

Try to eliminate the child's need to whine by really listening when the child properly asks for your attention.

Make sure that your child gets his or her share of focused attention every day. (SEE PAGE 183) Often the "whiniest" households are the ones where parents use the phrases, "In a minute!" or "Not now, Benjamin, I'm busy!" many times a day. These are legitimate phrases to use on occasion, but don't overdo it with a three-year-old. A minute is a long time when you're three.

I am personally convinced that whining is much less common among children whose parents provide brief but intense and readily responsive attention when the child needs it. This seems to "immunize" the child so that he or she is better able to resist the whining virus.

Negativity/Oppositional Behavior

ParenTips:

- *Remember That Oppositional Behavior in Young Child Is Normal—It Does Not Herald Future Delinquency!*

- *Opposition Represents the Child's Development of a Sense of Self and Autonomy.*

- *Do Not Reinforce Oppositional Behavior With Negative Attention: No Nagging, Shouting, Pleading.*

- *Do Not Reinforce Oppositional Behavior by Being Tentative.*

- *Use the "Effective Command."*

- *Accept the Parenting Role of "Dictator" When Necessary— It's Your Job!*

- *If Oppositional Behavior Persists or Becomes Overly Frequent, Change Your Behavior:*
  Figure out what makes you lose your cool.
  Before you explode or drop, **Stop!**
  Decide what's non-negotiable.
  When it's non-negotiable, **Only Say It Once.**

- **There are Three Ways to Change Chronic Obnoxious Behavior in Your Child.**

  The **Carrot** (keep chart and reward for "good behavior").

  The **Stick** (withhold privileges).

  Ask the Child: "What can you do to end this problem?"

- **Avoid Power Struggles At All Costs.**

  Develop "tricks" to use when child says, "You can't make me!" Stay calm, bargain, even bribe, but win!

We cannot expect our children to like everything we do, willingly obey every directive, docilely go along with every suggestion, or always be in a good mood.

Even young babies have feelings of their own—they may not want to be in a car seat or get dressed just now. Generally young children want to please us, but they may be having a bad day. And, of course, as preschoolers mature and become more independent, they must try out their autonomy much as a young bird must flap its wings before flying.

Some parents want so hard to please their children that they forget they have both the right and the responsibility to socialize the child. These parents feel that they are supposed to make every moment of the child's life happy and to eliminate every possible source of unhappiness. Such parents think, "If I'm just a clever enough parent, I'll figure out how to convince Alex to let me give him his medicine!"

Sometimes we have to strap a crying baby or screaming toddler in the car seat because we must go and we cannot leave the child behind. Remember parents do not have the power to make or keep their child happy all the time. We can't always convince a crying or screaming child to stop making those awful noises and smile in order to make things easier for us. But we always have the responsibility to keep our children safe.

Oppositional behavior and negativity are ***absolutely normal behaviors.*** They do not herald future delinquent behavior. They occur when children express their own feelings and try to exert their own will independent of what the parent does. But all oppositional behavior can be reinforced by the way the parents behave.

Two types of reinforcement can occur. The parent may provide much **too much attention** to the misbehaving child. Whether you nag, shout, cajole, plead, or beg, you are providing lots of attention—albeit negative attention.

Another type of reinforcement happens when parents are **tentative**. ("Should I really have this struggle over the car seat with Katie or should I call Grandma and tell her we're not coming?") Clever Katie quickly senses you are wavering but if you let her win now she will become a champion player of the game called Make Mommy Change Her Mind. If the child wins a few times, the game becomes part of the child's repertoire.

If you want your child to obey, follow these guidelines:

- Minimize the number of issues that are "non-negotiable." Let the child choose what color pants to wear, but not whether to get in the car seat.

- Use the **Effective Command:** "Jody, you may not hit your brother! Stop!" (SEE PAGE 30).

- Don't raise your voice but do speak emphatically and sternly. Parents who use these techniques tell me it actually helps to lower the volume of the voice while speaking very precisely.

- If the child protests or persists in the behavior, either say "This is non-negotiable, Jody!" or repeat the effective command.

- Do not be upset if the child cries. Your job is to teach the child the rules of behavior, not to prevent unhappiness.

Dictate when we must and negotiate when we can is the hallmark of good parenting.

When the Kids Don't Mind

What should parents do with children who have learned that they can get two things from their parents by being oppositional: **attention** and **power?**

You already know that negative attention is still attention. Discovering he or she can "get your goat" or make you lose your cool gives the child power.

Parents can change this situation only by changing **their own behavior:**

- Figure out what situations "get your goat." What makes you lose your cool? Are you tired? Does your child's behavior remind you of yourself as a child?

- Resolve that you will not lose your cool. My slogan for parents: "Before You Explode or Drop, STOP!" To make this work you must get in touch with your own feelings and learn what it feels like when you are heating up. Before you reach the boiling point, leave the room or count to twenty or take a few deep breaths.

- Keep to a bare minimum the issues that require obedience. This does not mean you should let the child be in charge. To the contrary. You stay in control by deciding in advance what is really important like safety rules, not hitting, etc. Tell your child these issues are non-negotiable and that if he or she does not obey the rules there will be consequences.

- When you do mean it, remember to say it *only once* and to say it in your softest but sternest voice while standing close to your child. "Jessica you may not hit your brother!" (The **Effective Command,** again).

If your child does not obey when it really matters, do not argue, try to explain or reason with the child, or give in until you are so exasperated that you scream. Instead, quietly and coldly and sternly tell the child that a rule has been broken.

Time-out in a boring place for one minute per year of age is a suitable punishment. Alternatively, you can withhold a privilege, like staying up late on a special occasion or going to the mall with you.

You can also keep a chart and reward your child for "good" behavior. At the end of a week in which the chart shows that the child has been obedient most of the time, there will be a reward. At this age activity rewards are best: a special trip to the zoo or to Mommy's office, but material rewards like a new book also work.

Ask your child to solve the problem. With children as young as five, having a meeting, just like you would at work can do the trick. Pick a neutral setting like a restaurant. Tell your child that you are upset because of the oppositional behavior. **Ask your child how he or she thinks the problem can be solved.** Stop talking and listen. When children realize parents are serious and really want their input they often come up with good solutions.

Don't worry about how your child will turn out. Because you have to say something umpteen times does not mean your child is becoming a delinquent. It means the child has learned you don't mean it the first time.

Remember that less is more. The fewer non-negotiable issues you have, the fewer times you have to tell your child something, and the lower the volume of your voice, the better.

Older Children Who Are Oppositional

What can you do when your child looks you in the eye and says, "You can't make me!"?

Everybody loses when there is a parent-child power struggle. If you win, the child is resentful. If the child wins, he or she feels bad. Kids know they aren't supposed to call the shots.

My bottom line advice is to **avoid power struggles.**

Doesn't that sound easy? Sometimes as I sit at my computer I think about how much easier it is to give advice than it is to parent! But the strategies I am about to suggest *do work.* Not every thing will work every time but knowing about these strategies can make parenting easier for you.

Prevent the problem! Don't take the children to the store if you know how much they hate tagging along when you do errands. The children feel useless. Maybe you feel that way when your husband is looking at gadgets in the hardware store; you'd rather be somewhere else.

Strategize. Can you figure out a way to avoid the situation that sets up the power struggle? Can a neighbor watch your child while you shop? Can you wait until Dad comes home?

Involve your child in the activity, the decision and problem-solving. Kids like to feel needed and valued. Even though it took extra work, when my children were seven or so I divided the grocery list and gave each child a shopping task. Obviously I had to go back when the child picked the wrong product or size. But they learned. They also learned to write on the refrigerator grocery list (organized into sections like groceries, produce, cleaning supplies) when we were running low on something.

If you say, "I know you don't like to come to the market but I have to shop and I can't leave you alone. When can we do this?" your child becomes involved in the decision. Try letting the child, within reason, pick the time. This kind of "power"—the decision-making kind—is heady for kids.

Develop a bag of parental tricks to use when the child says, "no! you can't make me!"

Stay calm and admit you're in a bind. Admit to the child, "Of course I can't make you, you're a big boy. I couldn't carry a big boy like you!" Sometimes this works and you'll get a reluctant, "All right—I'll come with you but I don't want to!" Allow the child negative feelings and grumbling as long as the action is positive and the power-struggle is averted.

Bargain with the child. Many parents, feeling that parents must win just because they are the parents, think bargaining is wrong. Bargaining is a variation of Grandma's rule: "If you do X, you will get Y." "I know you hate this but you are big enough to understand I must shop. If you come with me this time and show me you are big enough to be responsible, next time I will let you stay home alone," or "We will get a frozen yogurt on the way home."

Helpful hint: Don't use bargaining or bribing too often because the clever child may become oppositional just to get the award or concession. But used once in a while, the bargaining strategy works.

In summary there are three strategies parents can use when a child exhibits repetitive, oppositional, annoying, or disrespectful behavior: the **Carrot** (gold star and reward), the **Stick** (withhold privileges) and **Ask the child to solve the problem.**

In order for the carrot and stick to work you have to **mean it. NO** gold star unless the child deserves it and no wiggling out of a sanction because the child begs and pleads and promises to be good. Although consistency is not always 100 percent possible, when you are trying to modify behavior consistency is essential. I never said parenting was easy!

Talking Back

ParenTips:

- *Decide What Kind and Amount of "Sass" You Will Tolerate.*

- *Remember Your Child Has the Right to Express All Feelings.*

- *Rights End When Another Person (Including You) Gets Hurt.*

- *Use Time-Out or Some Other Sanction EVERY Time the Talking Back Occurs.*

- *Don't Let Your Children Watch Disrespectful TV—They Learn from It.*

Talking back, sassing parents, and name-calling are part of growing up. Every child does it. Children have always done it. Even in the "good old days" when children were more respectful they did it. The difference was they were punished for it, while today most parents ignore stuff that would have meant a trip to the woodshed.

Most parents want, deserve, and think they are entitled to respect. But many parents don't realize it takes work to raise a respectful child. And parents resent it when their kids are respectful to others, like teachers, while they have to put up with a lot of lip at home.

Parents also feel their children should be able to express themselves. Today's parents don't really want kids who say, "Yes, ma'am/ No, Sir" automatically but never think for themselves.

We don't train our children like dogs to sit and stay. We raise our children to think for themselves.

But no parent wants to be sassed, especially in front of others, and every parent gets tired of frequent or continuous backtalk.

There is a difference between a child saying heatedly, "I hate you!" and a child saying, "You bitch!" to Mother who has just said to turn the TV off.

Although both statements are theoretically disrespectful, saying you hate your mother in a fit of anger is expressing a feeling. The answer (as calmly as possible) is, "I'm sorry you feel that way. But the TV stays off."

Name calling reaches an intolerable level of disrespect and should be handled differently. Express **your** feelings first. "That word hurts me!"

Then mete out the appropriate punishment: time-out or withholding of a privilege like TV. Be sure to tell your child, and enforce it, that every time that word is used the child will be punished.

What about less nasty name calling? For some reason all preschoolers quickly pick up on two words to call their parents when they are angry at them, even if the words do not apply: *fat* and **dumb.**

These words are used a lot on TV and even very young kids pick up on the fact that they are insulting.

Parent's choice here. If the words bother you, use the sanctions mentioned. If they don't bother you, ignore them. It's still a good idea to limit TV! Alternatively you can make a joke, "If you think I'm fat you should see how fat the hippopotamus was—the one I took to school when I was your age." What does this humor do? First it defuses your child's anger. Second, the next time the child wants to call you fat, there may be a reconsideration of what word to use.

Because so much disrespectful behavior is seen on TV—even the "good" kind of children's TV—pay attention to what your preschoolers are watching. And tell the children that nice people don't do that even though it's on TV.

Temper Tantrums

ParenTips:

- *Do What You Can to PREVENT Frustration.*

- *Use Environmental Control So You Don't Have to Always Say, "No!"*

- *Try Clever Distraction.*

- *Speak Softly to Provide a Calming Effect.*

- *Give Choices When You Can.*

- *Don't Try to Reason. Just Say, "The Rule is No Hitting!"*

- *Don't Have Tantrums Yourself—Show the Child Grown-Up Ways to Deal with Anger.*

- *Provide EXTERNAL CONTROL (Hold Tightly) When Child under One Year Has a Tantrum.*

- *IGNORE Tantrum in an Older Child.*
  Walk away if child safe.
  Use "attention-less hold" if in public—hold child facing away from you, don't talk, just remove child from the scene.

- *Teach Your Child How to Deal with Anger.*
  Give strong feelings a name.

Teach anger-busting techniques—pound a pillow or march around
the room.

Help older children express anger in words or drawings.

- ## *DO NOT GIVE IN!*

Frustration and Its Consequences

Frustration is an inescapable part of life. Parents cannot provide a frustration-proof life for their children. All you can do is patiently teach your child how to deal with frustration.

Think about what it means to be a two-year-old child. You have mastered the art of mobility but still can't reach everything you want to get at. You don't have the muscle skills or dexterity to do all the things you want to do. You don't have the verbal skills to make your wishes known, and you certainly don't have the verbal skills to express how you are *feeling.* You have no idea how to handle frustration and anger except to "throw a fit."

Almost all day long some big person tells you to do something you don't want to do, like get undressed for bed, or stop doing something that is fun to do, like pulling the cat's tail.

Basically, a tantrum occurs because the child lacks self-control and the verbal ability to express feelings, does not have the skills to substitute a pout for an all-out tantrum, does not yet have a sense of what limits mean or what danger is, and does not yet have an understanding of the rights and desires of others.

During the second year of life a child is busy developing autonomy and independence. Children now want to do everything for themselves and call all the shots. Enough of this boring life where Mom does everything for me! But young children lack the skills they need to be independent and the wisdom to handle independence. So, for example, when you don't allow your child to play with the stereo, the child may explode in frustration.

It's fascinating to watch a tantrum in a toddler. Typically the child's rage is diffuse, not well coordinated, and it is directed toward himself or herself. The child may be furious at another child who has taken away a toy, but he or she slams down on the floor and kicks out at the air. It requires more maturity for the toddler to strike out at the one causing the frustration!

107

Prevention

1. In order to help your child learn to deal with frustration and accept limits, start by providing **environmental control.** Arrange things so that young children can't hurt what they get into and what they get into can't hurt them.

   My advice to parents who are childproofing their house is "Lock up, high up!" Sometimes it's a big pain but I promise that this is not forever. I know one set of parents who boxed up the CDs and stereo. Another family moved the valuable electronics to the the master bedroom which they keep locked.

2. **Distraction** is a another valuable strategy for helping frustration-prone children. Your child likes turning knobs? Consider providing an old radio with the insides taken out. Always have new toys and books squirreled away for emergencies.

3. Do what you can to **prevent fatigue** which makes all of us more susceptible to the effects of frustration. Be sure your child gets plenty of rest and snacks. Fatigue and hunger promote and enhance negative emotions like anger. Little kids may not want to nap or eat because they think they'll miss something, but it's up to you to schedule quiet times and snacks anyway.

4. If you sense your child is about to explode, **speak softly** and move slowly and soothingly. Try to keep the pace slow and easy.

5. Give **advance warning** that something like getting ready for bed is going to happen.

6. Give **choices** whenever you can to enhance the child's feeling of autonomy.

7. Try to **avoid the word "No!"** You can do this in two ways: catch 'em being good and say "Yes!" whenever you can ("Yes, we'll go to the park after lunch." instead of "No, we can't go now.")

8. **Don't try to reason** with a two-year-old or explain why he can't, for example, hit. Explanations just confuse the child. All you have to get across is that hitting is not allowed.

9. **Be a good role model.** Don't have tantrums yourself, but be sure your child knows that you do get angry and sees you handling your anger in healthy ways. It is important that the child learn what anger is and what it feels like. The very controlled household where no one ever seems angry is not the best place to raise a child. The child has to learn that it's always OK for people to feel anger or even rage but that it's never OK to act out this rage.

What to Do When a Tantrum Strikes

What you should do when a child has a tantrum depends on the age of the child. The under-eighteen-month-old child who is frantically out of control needs the **external control** you can provide by **holding the child tightly** and speaking softly until the child is over it. The tricky part is to provide external control without giving in to the child's demands. If you give in it teaches your children to throw a fit every time they want something they can't have.

The treatment for two- and three-year-old tantrum-throwers is to **ignore the tantrum.** Walk away—after making sure the child is safe—in order to physically remove your attention from the child. You should say something like, "I'll be back when you get control of yourself."

If the child is in a public place or in any danger, use the "attention-less hold". This is simply a way of holding children to help them with control while you keep them facing away from you. Your job is to provide **control without attention** so don't talk. It's OK to say, "I'll talk to you after you calm down," but don't try to cajole the child into stopping. That is the child's job.

What do you do when your two-year-old throws a tantrum in the cookie aisle of the market because you won't buy any? The rule is to ignore the tantrum but, because it's hard to let your child kick and scream on the floor of a public place, leave your cart right there. Use the "attention-less hold" to take the child out of the store until the fit is over.

Tantrums in Older Children

Usually by the time a child is three or so, tantrums are a thing of the past. You can delay this maturation by paying attention to the tantrum or you can speed it up by helping the child learn to verbalize anger. "Use words, Andrew. Tell me what is making you so angry!"

Six-year-olds may still exhibit tantrums but the frequency is much less and a tantrum is almost always associated with fatigue. By the time a child is seven, he or she tries very hard to be in control of everything, including temper.

But older children also have anger and frustrations. What do they do with it? Some ten-year-olds handle anger at friends by hitting, but Tens also yell or name-call and many will leave the scene to cool off. By the time a child reaches the teen years, physical hitting is pretty much replaced with verbal retorts, often sarcastic and mean.

Frequent temper tantrums in the school-age child are a cause for concern and should be reported to the pediatrician. Similarly, violent outbursts in a teenager may be a sign that something is wrong. Adults should not have temper tantrums but, of course, we sometimes do. Everybody has a breaking point.

My advice for adults who have trouble handling their anger is to take a "parental time-out." Remove yourself from the situation, take a few deep breaths, do some relaxation exercises, and figure out how you are going to handle whatever sent you to the brink. Remember my slogan: "Before you Explode or Drop, STOP!" Like children, adults get frustrated when they are fatigued. Parents must learn to get in touch with their own feelings so they can recognize when they are near the boiling point.

Start early to **teach your child about anger.** Anger is a human emotion. It protects us from being trampled by other people. It gave the caveman the adrenaline he needed to protect his food from marauders. But all of us must learn to discharge anger in a socially acceptable way. One of the best gifts parents can give a child is an understanding of anger and how to handle it.

1. **Give it a name:** "You feel angry because your brother won't give you the truck. I understand how you feel but you can't throw things."

2. Show your child how to **get rid of anger in appropriate ways,** like pounding a pillow (you can buy a special "anger pillow" to whack). Or show the child how to march around the room stomping up and down. Using big muscles, as in exercise, helps diffuse anger and stress. Some parents object because they say this will teach the child how to be angry. Not so. Children will figure out how to be angry on their own; this merely gives them techniques for expressing life's inevitable angers in a socially-appropriate manner.

3. Help older children **express their angry feelings** by drawing pictures of the feelings. Teach your child to scream in the shower to "let it all out" or to write angry thoughts on a piece of paper and then tear it into tiny pieces.

The most important thing a parent must learn about temper and tantrums is, no matter what the child's age, **DO NOT GIVE IN!** There is no quicker way of creating a child-sized monster.

Swearing/"Bathroom Talk"

ParenTips:

- ● *Don't Laugh, Punish Harshly, or Use Such Words Yourself.*
  Laughing reinforces cussing.

- ● *Don't Spank or Punish or Make Child Repeat Word.*

- ● *Do Ignore When You Can.*

- ● *Be Sure Child Knows Which Words Are Unacceptable.*

- ● *Whisper, "We Don't Use That Word."*

- ● *Use Time-Out for Repeated Offenses.*

- ● *Teach Substitute Words.*

- ● *Limit and Monitor TV.*
  That's where the bad words are.

All children go through a phase when they use "bad" language. This behavior used to be most prevalent at about age four. These days, because most children are in preschool of some sort and all children have access to TV, the bad words pop out earlier, truly out of the mouths of babes.

Preschoolers are for a brief time absolutely obsessed with naughty language, especially "bathroom" terms. They love saying things like, "You're a piece of pooh-pooh!" to peers and grown-ups alike. They consider such phrases clever and witty. They seem to know—or quickly learn—that these terms have the power to shock people and they revel in this power. Think about it. If you were only three years old and weren't very powerful, wouldn't it be fun to get people to react, or overreact, just using words!

Most children tire of these expressions soon. They learn that pleasing people gets them further than shocking people. But while the child is going through this phase parents have a dilemma. They instinctively realize that they should not call undue attention to these words because the kids get such a kick out of shocking grown-ups with them. But parents also tell me, "I don't want my kids to talk like this."

What to do? One woman told me that when she or her sister uttered a bathroom word, her mother made them sit in the bathroom. An appropriate sanction!

Here are the Heins' Do's and Don't's for dealing with bad language in preschoolers:

- **Don't** spank the child for using bad language.

- **Don't** wash the child's mouth out with soap—that never worked (except to enrich soap manufacturers). Anything that hurts or humiliates children makes them angry. Angry children are not in the right mood to learn about future behavior. Also, hurt or humiliated children come to feel they must be terrible or their parents wouldn't hit them or force them to eat something that tastes horrible.

- **Don't** use four-letter words yourself. We live in a casual and less-than-formal society. Often parents don't realize how lax they have become about their own language until they hear their child repeat some of the words.

- **Don't** ever laugh or act as though the words are cute. Bad language is *not cute!* As a matter of fact its use bespeaks ignorance and rudeness. When we consider how many wonderful and descriptive words there are in our language that derives from so many languages, it's dumb to describe all people and objects using only one or two Anglo-Saxon terms! If you really want to insult somebody, browse through the dictionary until you find just the right derogatory word!

When my own grandson came up with some shockers, it was hard not to giggle because it is so ludicrous to hear these words from a toddler. But parents must make a real effort not to laugh, because that will reinforce the tendency to use the words again. Three- and four-year-olds love an audience and love to get a reaction out of grown-ups.

- **Don't** ever scream, "Don't use the word _____!"

- **Don't** make the child repeat the offending words one hundred times or until the timer goes off. This is supposed to make the word lose its offending power or make the child so bored that he or she will never use the word again. The trouble is that this method doesn't work. And the logic is terrible—why should a parent make a child say a word over and over again if the parent wants the child to stop using the word?

What can parents **Do** to stop or at least minimize their child's use of unacceptable language?

- **Do** ignore bad language when you can. If you can stand it, pay no attention to the silly bathroom talk. If it upsets you, quietly tell the child not to use those words, without making too big a fuss, which only adds to the child's sense of "word power".

- **Do** make sure the child understands which words are acceptable. When you hear an offending word for the first time, quietly kneel down and whisper something like. "We don't use that word in our family." The intimate whisper often intrigues the child and the word is not used again or not as often.

- **Do** use appropriate discipline if the bad language gets out of hand. Today children hear totally unacceptable language on TV or around the neighborhood. If your four-year-old is in the habit of using such words, put the child in time-out. Here is one place it is suitable to use a warning because children may not know that they have used an offensive word—after all it was on TV. "That word is never acceptable. If you use it one more time you must go into time-out!" If the word pops out again, put the child in the time-out place. When the timer goes off, tell the child, "The rule is no swearing. If you use that word, then you must be timed-out."

- **Do** teach the child substitute words. You can play a silly name-calling game together. "You're a squashed banana!" or "You're a burnt marshmallow!" The sillier, the better.

- When children are old enough to understand, **explain** how people are hurt by name-calling. Evoke the children's empathy by asking how they would feel if that word were used to describe them.

- **Do** monitor and limit TV. If your child hears people on TV using unacceptable words, use the opportunity to say, "We don't use those words. There are zillions of words people can use instead. Let's think of some or look in the dictionary."

Dawdling

● *Avoid Rushing!*

    Try not to rush yourself!

    Try not to rush your young children.

    Prepare everything the night before.

● *Make Dressing as Easy as Possible.*

    Easy-on clothes.

    Make a game out of dressing quickly.

● *Maintain Routines.*

● *Use Rewards Rather Than Reminders.*

    Don't constantly remind child to hurry.

    Constant prodding builds up absent-mindedness.

Dawdling is a common and frustrating problem.

Young children dawdle because they are not completely skilled at focusing their attention on a task and they do not yet have a good sense of time or what time is.

A two-year-old may say, "Mommy has to get to work on time." But even if the child is old enough to pronounce the words the child has no idea what "on time" means or why being late can be a problem.

There are two additional reasons preschoolers dawdle. First of all, they can be overwhelmed when Mommy is rushing and the entire household is in a tizzy. The more you rush, the more they feel overwhelmed and the slower they get.

Second, young children have an uncanny ability to sense the very thing that upsets us the most. Though they might not be able to define "power," they probably get a kick out of having the power to make Mom lose her cool. After all, most of the time she's the one in control.

These days there are millions of mothers of preschoolers in the work force. This means there are millions of mothers out there being "driven crazy" by a dawdling child. I can well remember trying to get two preschoolers ready for school so that I could get to the hospital on time. I can still feel the anxiety. Was this the day I wasn't going to be able to pull it off?

Over the years I've learned a few anti-dawdling tricks, which I wish I had known when my own children were dawdling. None of these are absolutely sure-fire "cures," but all of them can help get the problem under control.

Avoid Rushing!

1. Be prepared ahead of time! Set out clothes the night before and gather together all the things your child will need to take to school—from permission slips to birthday cupcakes. Lay out your own clothes and gather what you will need in your briefcase as well. Anything that keeps you from rushing in the morning will help the atmosphere in the house and that in turn will help the dawdling problem.

2. Build some **extra time** into your morning schedule so that the inevitable unexpected can be accommodated.

3. Try to **keep the morning pace slow,** as slow as is humanly possible, so that your child will not feel rushed.

Make Dressing as Easy as Possible

1. Buy clothes that are easy to put on. If your child is not skilled at dressing, help the child. Some parents struggle because they have two conflicting goals: being on time and teaching the child how to be self-sufficient. Heins's suggestion: Be on time during the week and teach the child self-care on weekends.

2. Make a game out of what would otherwise be a grim situation. My young cousin cured my son of dawdling when getting ready for bed by inventing

a game called "Break the World's Record!". He told my son that the last person who broke the world's record got undressed in five seconds and challenged my dawdler to beat the record. Amid much hilarity with a stop watch, my son got undressed and into his pajamas in "record" time.

Maintain routines so your child knows what to expect when: wash up, get dressed, breakfast, brush teeth, put on jacket, etc.

Use Rewards Rather Than Reminders

1. A **timer** can be used to play "Beat the Timer" ("Let's see if you can get dressed before the bell rings!") or to tick away to remind the child of the task of getting dressed.

2. Try "Grandma's Rule." This is a simple proposition: If you do X, you will earn Y. "If you get dressed on time today, you will have time to play with your train before you go to school."

3. There's always the old Gold Star Reward System. Award a star every morning the child is dressed on time. When the child has earned a whole week of stars, give a treat or small toy. Don't forget the very best reward can be special time with a parent.

4. Don't encourage dawdling by constantly telling your child to "Hurry up!" Dr. Spock (page 492) says, "It's easy to fall into the habit of prodding children and this can build up an absentminded balkiness in them. Parents say they have to nag or the child won't get anywhere. It becomes a vicious circle, but the parent usually starts it, especially an impatient parent or one who doesn't leave enough time to allow for children's naturally slow pace."

Avoid all the **won't works** like yelling, cajoling, nagging, threatening.

Give yourself—and the kids—a break on weekends by slowing down the household pace.

Although peak dawdling takes place before age three, which is a bit young for problem-solving, an older child will often come up with ingenious answers if asked to figure out a way to get everybody out of the house on time in the morning.

It's permissible to leave the child behind (not alone, of course!) once or twice. Kids hate being left out. Nothing teaches the concept of consequences better than having the child experience one.

Pouting/Sulking

ParenTips:

- *Don't Expect Your Child to Be Happy All the Time.*

- *Remember There Are Things Parents Cannot Make Children Do:*
    Eat.
    Poop.
    Fall asleep.
    Be happy.

- *Don't Feel Guilty If Your Child Pouts or Sulks.*
    Everybody's entitled to a sulk.

- *Acknowledge Your Child's Feelings.*
    "I'm sorry you're unhappy...."

- *Do Not Give In—Let 'Em Sulk.*

- *Ignore Most Sulking and Pouting.*

- *Send Child to the "Pouting Chair" If Behavior Is Continuous.*

Parents do not like to see their children *look unhappy* or *act unhappy.* But all children pout or sulk on occasion.

Pouting is making a face of displeasure. This is an early weapon of preschool children and it's usually directed at Mommy or another caretaker who is not doing what the child wishes or is putting unwelcome sanctions on the tot's behavior.

Sulking is related to pouting but is the weapon of older children, usually of school age. It is the unhappy face plus unhappy body language plus often under-the-breath grumbling: "My Mom *never* lets me do anything I want to do!" The goal of the child is to be sure everybody around knows he or she is unhappy.

Those about to become parents have fantasies about their unborn children. Nobody ever fantasizes a crying, whining, pouting, or sulking child. The child of our dreams is always happy and smiling.

But there is a reality of parenting. No matter how much we want it, and no matter how hard we try, and no matter how good we are at parenting tasks, we cannot make our children happy all of the time. Nobody can control the way anybody feels—not even oneself! And, of course, nobody is happy all of the time.

Nonetheless we want to feel proud of ourselves as parents, even in the face of the inevitable challenges and frustrations of parenting. We want to be good parents, we want our children to consider us good parents, and we want the world to acknowledge that we are good parents.

So if a child pouts or sulks, especially in public, we think the whole world sees us as lousy parents. And that hurts!

Even if nobody's watching we may take the pouts and sulks to heart; we have done or are doing something wrong. And, of course, we feel guilty. We automatically, almost reflexively, blame ourselves for every moment of minor unhappiness our child demonstrates.

Don't feel guilty because of a pout or a sulk. Guilt does not enhance parenting; it detracts from it. Don't let your child's gestures upset you. Do not feel responsible for such demonstrated unhappiness.

Everybody is entitled to feeling unhappy and showing it. Even my dogs pout when I tell them to "kennel-up" in the middle of a game. But pouting behavior which persists or recurs frequently is almost always reinforced by the parent's reaction.

If the pouting bothers you too much and you try to get it to stop, your child quickly figures out that parental attention—and perhaps even parental capitulation about an issue—is forthcoming. Ergo, continued pouting. It works!

Try a new technique. **Acknowledge the feeling** in a noncommittal way: "I'm sorry you're unhappy about having to go to bed before your brother. He is older. When you get bigger you will be able to stay up longer." Use a friendly but not overly sympathetic tone of voice (the same tone you would use to politely get rid of a salesperson from whom you had no intention of making a purchase). And **don't give in.**

After you have made your statement, **ignore** the pouting. If the pouting is virtually continuous, tell your child that pouting (like whining) makes other people unhappy. The rule is that the child will have to go to the "pouting chair" until he or she can put on a happy face.

Be sure the child understands the difference between the two faces. Have a session in front of the mirror where you exaggerate showing how to pout and how to look happy. This mirror session often leads to giggles and you get the happy face without resorting to the chair.

The message you want to convey is that it's OK to have negative feelings and you understand why your child has them. But when the sad face makes others feel bad, the child must choose between stopping this behavior or being alone for a while.

Interrupting

- *Model and Teach Rules of Conversation.*

- *Say, "It's My Turn." Rather than "Don't Interrupt!"*

- *Adults Have a Right to Have a Conversation Without Interruption.*

- *Don't Call a Child Rude or Punish; Patiently Repeat the Rules.*

- *Teach Telephone Courtesy: Adults Are Not to Be Interrupted Unless the Matter is Urgent—and Role-Play What "Urgent" Is.*

- *Don't Sweat It—This Behavior Will Go Away.*

A young child who is mastering language is enthralled with its power and glory but hasn't had a chance to learn all the rules. When they figure out a way to express something that is exciting or important to them they may explode with speech.

Young children interrupt when we are talking to them because they are so excited about what they have to say they can't hold it in. They are so new at language they are afraid that if they don't say it **right now** they'll forget. They haven't yet learned the polite conventions of conversation that gives each speaker a turn. And they are egocentric and are convinced that **what they have to say is the most important thing in the world.**

This kind of interrupting is developmental and will go away by itself, but not without some judicious parental intervention.

When children first learn to speak we parents are so proud and excited that we give the child the floor and encourage the child to speak. We defer our own speech in favor of our child's new talent.

Parents are understandably ambivalent. On the one hand we love our child's developing language skills and want to encourage talking. On the other hand we don't want the child to become an insufferable bore who never shuts up.

How and how often and when should we intervene? Rather than say something like, "Don't interrupt, Mark, it's not polite!" to a two-year-old who probably doesn't understand the meaning of "interrupt" or "polite," tell the child **what to do:** "Wait! It's Mommy's turn to talk now! Wait until I get through."

You don't have to say this every time. Your child best learns the rhythm of speech by **observation** and **listening.** Your abstract comments about why polite people don't interrupt are pretty useless.

Children must also be taught that adults have a right to have a conversation among themselves without being interrupted. When something needs to be said , the child must learn to preface a legitimate interruption thus: "Excuse me. I can't reach the peanut butter. Can you please get it down for me." Learning this preface and what constitutes an important reason to interrupt, takes time.

When You Are Talking on the Telephone

Another kind of interrupting occurs when adults are talking on the telephone and the child wants you **right now!** Interrupting when a parent is on the telephone must rank high on the list of annoying things preschoolers do.

When my own children were little they seemed to be able to play together quietly and without my participation until the phone rang or I picked up the phone to make a call. Then they wanted me—right at that moment!

We once had a parrot that would talk quietly to himself all day long. But the minute I got on the phone, Papagayo started screaming. I can only conclude that the telephone triggers annoying behavior in more than one species!

What mysterious thing happens when Mommy talks on the telephone? For one thing she is not paying attention to the children. Mommy is focusing her attention on something else.

Parents have to teach what I call "household manners," those social niceties that enable a family to live in peace and harmony in one dwelling. One of these niceties is to keep quiet or leave the room when someone is on the phone.

A few suggestions to help minimize interruptions when you are on the phone, talking with others, or busy with work requiring concentration— like paying bills to meeting a deadline on the computer :

You are the **grown-up in charge** and you have a right to visit with friends or do your work uninterrupted.

Avoid negative attention to interrupting children. No threats, yelling, cajoling, screaming.

When you know you don't want to be disturbed, tell the children you can only be interrupted for an **urgent message.** Role-play with the children so they will understand what "urgent" means.

When the child interrupts you, quietly leave the circle or excuse yourself on the telephone. Privately, so the child does not sense he or she is being corrected in front of others, tell the child you are busy and will talk later.

Keep a special **timer** near the telephone for when you expect long conversations—as many parents who work at home do. Tell the child you will be through when the timer goes off.

Prevent problems by arranging to have things for the child to do when you are too busy to pay attention. One trick I used was to get a young teen sitter when I was having company so there was someone to play games with the children.

Another trick that may work in some houses is to have a designated "quiet place" in your house where the phone is located. The children can play in the quiet room but only quiet games: coloring, stickers, reading, etc. Boisterous games are played elsewhere.

You can try Grandma's Rule. Wise Grandma figured out that children respond better to carrots than sticks. "Children, if you let me talk to Aunt Sarah in peace and quiet, I will take you to get a frozen yogurt." If they do, you do. If they don't, you don't and you explain they are not getting the treat because they didn't.

If the child is close to five, try saying you get upset when you are interrupted and can't talk in peace. Ask the child if he or she can think of a way to keep quiet and not interrupt. Even a kindergartner can sometimes come up with a solution to such a problem. And because it is the child's solution it usually works.

Of course, there is no such thing as instant conversion from annoying behavior to good behavior so don't expect fast results.

Lying

- *Understand That "Fantasy Falsehoods" Are Not to Deceive You.*

  The child believes the falsehood.

  This is a normal developmental stage.

- *Gently Help Children Separate Truth from Reality.*

  Role-play the truth.

- *When Your Child Lies to Deceive You, Find Out the Underlying Reason and Deal with That, Not Just the Lie.*

- *Why Children Lie:*

  To avoid punishment or criticism.

  To get out of an obligation.

  To impress or con someone.

  To enhance their status.

- *Teach Children That Trust Is the Basis of Human Relationships.*

- *Don't Be Afraid to Use White Lies to Teach Children the Importance of Not Hurting People.*

Preschool Lies

Children tell two kinds of lies. I call these "preschool lies" and "school-age lies" for want of better terms and also because these lies are dependent on the child's level of development.

Preschool children are learning and practicing how to separate fantasy from reality. Preschoolers are also egocentric and truly believe it is their thoughts and wishes that cause things to happen.

The preschooler doesn't yet know what truth is, let alone have the ability to understand there can be shades of gray between the truth and a falsehood. Piaget teaches us that children are close to age seven before they really understand what a lie is and that lying is bad.

When your preschooler tells you a blatant lie—a "fantasy falsehood"— remember that the child is not really trying to deceive you. The child believes what he or she is saying and wants it to be true. "The baby said she wanted to go to the playground!" is an example. Of course the baby can't talk yet and Jimmie knows it. But he wants to go to the playground and has chosen this way of saying so. It makes perfect sense to the child that everybody should want to go to the playground.

Understand **why** the child tells such tales and use gentle guidance to **help the child learn to separate wish from reality.**

Ask, "How did the baby tell you that?" The child may tell you that the baby said "Goo-goo!" You can then ask, "And you think that means she wants to go the playground?" Sometimes the child will say, "Baby can't talk but I want to go to the playground and take her with me." Or the child may insist Baby said it, but at least you have started the process of focusing on reality.

Many of the stories children tell stem from their active daydreaming or fantasy life, which is very rich at this age. "There was this man who stole the ice cream out of the freezer and I drove Daddy's car to get the police!"

How should parents handle this kind of lying? Help your young child sort out reality from fantasy. Don't worry about the morals of lying yet. Don't reinforce lying by encouraging the child to repeat the cute story for Aunt Sarah. But don't deny the child the pleasure of the fantasy, either.

As a matter of fact you have two jobs: to encourage inventiveness *and* to help children realize there is a difference between what's in their heads and what is reality. Try a comment like, "What a clever story you made up!" rather than what we used to say, "Good boys don't lie!"

School Age Lies

Lying now is used by the child to deceive someone, just as lying by an adult is for the purpose of deception. The good news is that the child has matured to the point where he or she can tell an adult-type lie. The bad news is that you will likely become both angry and hurt when you realize that your child is lying to you.

All children will deliberately lie at one time or other. Children lie to **avoid punishment** or **criticism,** to **get out of** meeting an obligation, to **impress** someone, to **con** someone, or to enhance their **status.**

Some children will lie to test their parents. They want to check on whether lies are acceptable or not, or they want to see if their parents are paying attention to what they are saying.

Look for the reason. If the child is lying about homework, maybe there's trouble with school. If the child is lying about obedience to a house rule, perhaps there needs to be a family conference about rules and why they are hard to follow. If the child is lying to impress a friend, perhaps the child has a self-esteem problem. Your job is to figure out why the child is lying.

Never use entrapment to check for truthfulness. Instead of asking your son where he was and gleefully catching him in a lie, say you saw him playing video games at the mall when he was supposed to be doing his homework at the library. Ask the child to help you devise a logical and appropriate sanction for not being where he was supposed to be. Focus on the underlying broken rule, not the lie.

Trust

The important lesson you must teach your child is that lying hurts people because it destroys the basic contract of trust. The underlying thing the child is covering up is of importance to parents. But lying itself can hurt a child (nobody will trust a liar) as well as the person lied to. Lying hurts the people who trust us; robbery of trust is as serious as stealing any other prized possession.

"White Lies"

What should parents do about "white lies," those untruths we tell to avoid hurting someone's feelings?

How people feel about honesty varies from culture to culture. In Japan it is so important to preserve social harmony that it is virtually required that one avoid telling the truth if it would hurt someone's feelings. Western parents teach their children that any act of lying is bad.

All of us should learn to tolerate ambiguity. This complex world we live in can no longer be viewed as black and white—if indeed it ever could be. We have to teach our children two rules as they are growing up: **1) Tell the Truth** and **2) Don't Hurt People's Feelings.** And we have to teach them when to use each rule.

Explain that we don't say, "Your casserole tasted awful and we gave it to the dog!" Instead we say "Thank-you for sharing your new recipe with us!" When the child points out that you're not telling the truth, you have to explain that both truth and empathy are important.

One more suggestion: if you want a child to learn that the best life is lived by people who trust each other and value the truth, model that trust and truth for the child. **DON'T LIE TO YOUR CHILD.**

Worrisome Traits

Shyness

The Over-Compliant Child

Hyperactivity

Shyness

- *Extreme Shyness Is Genetic.*

- *Accept This Temperament Trait—You Won't Change It.*

- *Don't Get Emotionally Involved Yourself—Especially If You're Shy.*

- *Provide Strategies to Help Child Deal with Shyness:*
  Avoid overwhelming situations.
  Give child time to warm up.
  Rehearse new situations.
  Teach child how to make eye contact and speak firmly.

We once thought that shyness was a learned trait. We now know that extreme shyness has a genetic component.

About 15 percent of children are born with a tendency to be shy when confronted with new people and cautious when put in new situations.

The inhibited, or shy, child will exhibit actual, measurable physiological changes like an increase in heart rate and muscle tension when confronted with a new situation. These are the same changes experienced when adults are subjected to stress.

About 20 percent of children are the opposite of shy. These babies smile when they are confronted with something new and do not demonstrate the physiological changes mentioned. They go to a stranger happily and do not seek refuge behind the mother's skirts.

The majority of children are neither shy nor gregarious by nature but, like most of us, are sometimes shy and sometimes outgoing. The shy and gregarious infants and children, on the other hand, almost always demonstrate either the shy or gregarious behavior.

And these traits persist. The inhibited infant remains shy. Such children avoid the unfamiliar. They are quieter in play and talk less. They usually do well at school and are unlikely to have behavior problems or become delinquent, but are at a somewhat higher risk for anxiety disorders in adulthood.

Whether a child is temperamentally shy or gregarious seems to be inborn and not related to how the child is treated by the parents. Thus genes, rather than environment—nature, rather than nurture—seem to be the most important determinants.

Shyness can be disturbing to parents. The shy child seems uncomfortable and no parents want to see their child suffer.

Fathers are often upset because they equate a shy child, especially a boy, with being a "baby" or a "sissy," neither of which is acceptable. And parents of either gender who remember a shy childhood want desperately to prevent their child from experiencing the same distress.

Parents are unable to change the basic personality traits with which a child comes into the world. But parents can *help* a child deal with the hand already dealt. How?

- Understand and accept your child's personality.

- Remember you did not do anything to cause the shyness.

- Do not worry about the shy child's future and do not let your own memories of painful shyness or being called a "sissy" interfere with the way you parent the shy child.

- **Prepare** your child for **new situations.** Talk about a relative who is coming to visit. Explain you will meet Aunt Sue at the airport and she will sleep in the guest room.

- Structure your child's life to temper situations you know will be frightening. If a big family party is planned, take the child there early so he or she can get used to the site and meet new arrivals in small groups. This is easier on a shy child than arriving at a strange house filled with noisy strangers.

- Give your child **time to warm up** to new situations. Don't make things harder by forcing the child to kiss Cousin Sally or by acting disappointed when the child hangs back.

- Help your child master shyness. Enroll the child in preschool or make opportunities for the child to be with same-age children. Tell the teacher that the child is shy so you can work together to help the child deal with this.

- Praise the child specifically for the things he or she does well to build up a sense of confidence. Self-esteem depends largely on competence so give your child many opportunities to do the things he or she does well.

- Role-play together to help the child learn how to talk to people and meet new people. Tell your child to pretend to be a puppydog meeting a pussycat. "What would Puppydog say to Kittycat?" This is an important game to play because shy children talk less. When asked questions they answer politely but they don't make spontaneous comments. As adults they have trouble initiating conversations.

- Help the child **rehearse new things** like the first day of classes or going to a friend's birthday party.

- **Avoid labels.** Don't call your child shy or refer to your child as the "shy one." If you must say anything to people, say, "My child likes to look new people over very carefully."

The Over-Compliant or "Too Good" Child

ParenTips:

- *Encourage All Children to Express Their Feelings, Even Negative Ones.*

- *Don't Subject Daughters to "Little Girls Should Always Be Nice" Nonsense.*

- *Don't "Over-Reward" Good Behavior.*

- *Encourage "Safe Boldness" in Physical Excercise.*

Parents struggling with a typically non-compliant child may find it hard to believe that children can be too good.

But occasionally a child can be what we call over-compliant.

There are children who never seem to have any wishes of their own, never makes the kind of noises or messes you expect kids to make, don't seem to show any emotions like anger or sadness or fearfulness, don't question any of the parents' rules or directives, don't like to play with other children, and get along better with adults than peers. Such children can be described as *over-compliant*. These children are, indeed, too good for their own good!

There are perfectly benign causes of over-compliance. For example, parents may over-reward good behavior. Sometimes this can occur after a new baby arrives if parents overdo the praising of the older sibling's maturity.

Some young children respond to a frightening situation like a death, serious illness, or divorce by becoming overly well-behaved, because they think this will remedy the situation or prevent a recurrence. Sometimes a child will act excessively good because of feeling guilty about something in the hope that good behavior will atone for the wrong. Most of the time the guilt is in the child's imagination. One young boy I know thought he was responsible when his baby sister was hospitalized for croup because he had played rough with the baby the day before.

Insight into the behavior, along with appropriate reassurances, usually works and the child is back to a normal compliance level in no time—often too soon!

Sometimes the real or imagined trauma has caused damage to the child and counseling is indicated. Also, serious problems like depression, obsessive-compulsive disorder, schizophrenia, severe anxiety, and retardation can present with what looks like over-compliant behavior.

So, if your child is *really* too good *really* too often and you're worried about this symptom, tell your child's pediatrician. A psychological evaluation may be indicated.

Perfectionism in Girls

Sometimes without realizing it parents "over-reward" compliance in girls. We understand that "boys will be boys" but we expect girls to be "sugar and spice and everything nice."

When we tell a girl to be nice, what we expect is that she will be polite and compliant and conforming. In other words, **do what others expect.** The message is: Always please others, always put the needs and wants of others before your own needs and wants, always do what is expected of you. That's a good girl!

What makes a little girl want to be good? **Approval!** Little girls get their approval ratings from being good and sweet.

There's also some evidence that girls are more sensitive than boys to verbal clues. Girls are better at hearing other people's needs—so they respond to them better—and girls listen for other people's approval—and respond by becoming even "gooder."

Lots of little girls grow up to be perfectionists. They figure out early that they will be rewarded by doing everything expected of them in the best possible way. They also make themselves indispensable: "I'm the only one who can do this!" "It's all up to me!" "If I don't hold it together everything will fall apart!"

Perfectionism and indispensability ensure these women a life-time supply of approval. But it comes at a steep price.

Yes girls respond to verbal cues better than boys. But girls are still humans with wants of their own. Parents should encourage girls to express themselves, to stand up for themselves, to allow themselves to accept the care of others and to feel needy. And, of course, boys should be encouraged to express their feelings, even tearful ones. (SEE PAGE 74)

Hyperactivity

ParenTips:

- *Repeat after Me: Parenting Does Not Cause This.*

- *If You or a Teacher Suspect ADHD (Attention Deficit Hyperactivity Disorder) Get the Child to a Specialist in Behavioral Pediatrics—Fast.*

- *Don't Be Afraid to Use Medication If It Is Indicated.*

- *Learn Strategies for Managing the Child at Home and in Public.*

- *Work as a Team: Parents, Doctor, School, Child.*

- *Discover and Nurture the Child's Compensatory Strengths and Believe in Your Child.*

- *Do Not Confuse Exuberance in a Child with Hyperactivity. Never Use the ADHD Label or ADHD Medication Unless the Diagnosis Has Been Firmly Established by a Competent and Experienced Health Professional.*

Attention deficit hyperactivity disorder is real, it's fairly common, and it can cause much distress in the children involved as well as great turmoil in families.

This is not a new disorder; children with the symptoms of ADHD were described over one hundred years ago. The hyperactive child has also been described in children's literature ("Fidgety Phil/He won't sit still"). However the terminology used to describe these children has changed a good deal through the years (minimal brain dysfunction, the hyperkinetic child, etc.) The term used today is attention deficit hyperactivity disorder (ADHD).

How common is ADHD? Somewhere between 3 and 6 percent of the children in the U.S. have this disorder. Although the prevalence varies from study to study and country to country, all studies show that boys are more commonly involved than girls with a boy/girl ratio of about 6:1.

What are we talking about when we use the term attention deficit? When we attend to a task, our brain filters out other stimuli so that we can pay attention. The brains of people with ADHD can't do this filtering job very well.

A child with ADHD demonstrates excessive activity, poor sustained attention, problems with impulse control, and difficulty getting along with others.

Not all excessively active children have ADHD. To help everybody define ADHD the same way, a list of fourteen criteria is used. Because all children may show one or more of these behaviors at some time, a child must have had at least eight of the symptoms for at least six months in order for the diagnosis of ADHD to be made And, as with every other symptom complex, the problem may be mild, moderate, or severe.

Children with ADHD :

- are restless or fidgety,

- have difficulty staying in their seats,

- are easily distracted,

- have difficulty waiting their turn,

- blurt out answers to questions before they have been completed,

- have difficulty following instructions,

- have difficulty sustaining attention in tasks or play,

- often shift from one activity to another,

- have trouble playing quietly,

- may talk excessively,

- interrupt others frequently,

- don't seem to listen to what is being said,

- often lose things,

- may engage in dangerous activities without thinking of the consequences (run into the street without looking).

It is pretty obvious that **every child** will exhibit at least one of these behaviors sometime. Further, many of these behaviors are common in preschoolers. I stress this to underline the importance of **not labeling a child.** Don't, even in a joke, refer to your child as "hyperactive" unless the diagnosis has been made.

The problems of ADHD start early in life. But most toddlers are distractable and impulsive at least some of the time so that parents may be unaware that the child has a problem. By the time the child goes to school, everybody *knows* there is a problem. Looking at the criteria list, it's easy to see how much difficulty such a child would have learning—and how much difficulty the teacher would have teaching.

Thus poor school achievement, with or without concomitant learning disabilities, is a hallmark of the school age child with ADHD. Also, some children with ADHD may exhibit conduct problems like destructiveness, aggression, oppositional behavior, or lying and stealing. Many ADHD children have difficulties relating to their peers because they tend to be self-centered, emotionally immature, and unaware of consequences. And, of course, poor self-esteem results from under-achievement and poor peer relationships. ("I can't do it and nobody likes me!").

What causes ADHD? Nobody knows for sure. However there is a good deal of evidence that this problem has a biological basis. Twenty to 30 percent of parents and siblings also have symptoms of ADHD. One quarter of the biological parents of ADHD children have similar symptoms compared with 4 percent of adoptive parents.

Other evidence for a biological basis comes from studies of brain function indicating under-activity in certain parts of the brain. A recent study showed that brain glucose metabolism was significantly reduced in adults who had been hyperactive since childhood, especially in those regions of the brain involved in controlling attention and movement. There is no question that ADHD is due to an abnormality in the way the brain functions. Although the child with ADHD can develop compensatory strategies to improve behavior and learning, the child can't control the way his or her brain works.

Can ADHD be caused by "wrong" parenting? In my opinion, the answer is **No!** There are studies that show mothers of ADHD children are more negative and directive toward the hyperactive child, but it is likely that the mother's behavior results from having to deal with such a child, not that the ADHD was caused by her parenting.

Can anything be done for these children? **Yes,** to a degree. First of all the child needs an **accurate diagnosis,** which means the child needs a **comprehensive diagnostic evaluation** including psychological and educational evaluations.

A pediatrician knowledgeable about, and interested in, behavior problems in children is the best person to coordinate this diagnostic evaluation and make treatment recommendations to the school and family.

Medication can help many of these children. Ritalin, a stimulant, works on the brain to improve attention span and decrease impulsiveness. Although there are some side effects, I favor a trial of Ritalin for every child diagnosed with ADHD. The dosage must be carefully regulated and the medication must be carefully monitored. If the medication is helping, both parents and teachers will notice an improvement in the child's behavior and performance over a few weeks. Other medications such as antidepressants, can also be tried if Ritalin does not help.

Medication alone is *never* the answer. **Educational strategies, behavior modification,** and **counseling** therapy for the child and parents are all important parts of the treatment spectrum.

Parents must learn special management skills and strategies. Some recent books can help parents put this disorder into perspective, learn management strategies and techniques, and establish a parent/school partnership to maximize the child's performance. (SEE Suggested Further Readings.)

Support groups and classes or workshops about managing ADHD are also very useful to parents.

What happens to these children when they grow up? The hyperactivity often "calms down" in late adolescence. But many teens with ADHD still have difficulties with school and exhibit impulsive behavior. They may also develop antisocial behaviors, probably related to poor self esteem, school failures, and difficulty in making friends. Loss of motivation ("giving up") occurs in some and may lead to dropping out of school.

In many cases medication is stopped in adolescence but it should be continued even in adulthood if the doctor and patient feel it is helping.

If the educational strategies keep the child in school and the therapy helps the child realize he or she is **different but not bad or dumb,** there can be a very favorable outcome.

Although adults with ADHD still have abnormalities in brain activity and some behavioral difficulties, many are able to compensate for their "differences." They also can develop and exhibit what are called "redemptive features." For example, inattention to detail can be associated with greater ability to see the big picture. A study of ADHD adults showed that their employers rated them equally with control adults without ADHD on six out of seven questions about performance.

So the picture is not hopeless. Parenting an ADHD child is tough but with knowledge and support you can do it.

The Bright, Energetic Child Who Does NOT Have ADHD

What about the unbelievably active preschooler?.

Exuberance, energy, eagerness, curiosity are characteristics that are not only normal but desirable in a child. A child who is exuberant, energetic, eager, and curious should not be described as hyperactive.

But it's easy to see how normal "high" activity levels can be labeled as abnormal hyperactivity. "He's into everything!" can either describe an energetic, curious child or a child who is distractible and impulsive because of ADHD.

Because all toddlers and young children get into everything —it's part of normal development in children old enough to explore new things but too young to understand concepts of danger or possession—parents of young children with ADHD may think their child is merely active instead of hyperactive.

On the other hand, because there is so much written about ADHD, some parents have a tendency to read abnormality into the behaviors of a perfectly normal child. I hate labels, so I would never use the word "hyperactive" unless the child had been diagnosed with ADHD.

I know a wonderful three-year-old boy who is very bright and very energetic. Though he learns rules quickly he is so eager to tell visitors what he just saw or did that he cannot restrain himself. He knows polite people don't interrupt so when visitors are talking he says, "'Scuse me! 'Scuse me!" over and over again until he gets the floor.

One day I took him for a walk. He said, "See those red signs on the corner? My mommy says they say 'Caaalllm down,!'" What a clever mother to turn every stop sign into a message for her energetic preschooler!

Such bright/energetic children are best handled by accepting that they are what they are. Adaptive behavior is what's needed—on the part of the parents! It can take lots of parental ingenuity to keep up with such a child. You will become very adept at answering questions. One friend told me her young son watches the news on TV and then asks such questions as, "Will I get AIDS?" and "How long does it take to fly to Saudi Arabia?" She asked me, "Do you have any idea how hard it is to explain the news to a five-year-old?"

Become good friends with the children's librarian at your local library so you can have stimulating and interesting books available at all times. I could always calm my own children by getting out a new book—kept hidden for those moments when something new and stimulating was in order.

The real challenge is to keep one step ahead of the bright child. I have found these children are more apt to be frustrated by boredom than by tasks which stretch them slightly beyond their abilities. But don't push them or make them show off their brightness. Just recognize they are happiest when being challenged.

Accept your child, and accept the challenge. The rewards of living with a bright child can be great once you realize how to keep up. You'll never have a dull moment!

"Bad" Habits That Drive Parents Crazy

Thumb-Sucking

Nail-Biting

Nose-Picking

Thumb-Sucking

ParenTips:

- *Ignore Thumb-Sucking in Preschoolers.*

- *Never Punish or Tease Young Thumb-Sucker.*

- *Help the Motivated School-Age Child Who Wants to Stop.*
  Acknowledge child owns problem and solution.
  Try "aversive taste therapy."
  "Paradoxical" therapy may work.
  Gold star chart often helpful.
  Limit TV and other inactive times.
  Reassure—"Everybody stops."

Thumb-Sucking in Babies

Thumb-sucking is very common. It's the child's first "bad" habit. It worries parents, but it needn't.

Babies **need a lot of non-nutritive sucking.** Some babies need more than others. I think it's great when a baby finds and uses its thumb. This is the baby's first act of independence! Now self-comfort is possible; Mother becomes a bit less necessary.

It is perfectly normal and perfectly OK for babies and young children to suck the thumb while falling off to sleep or when feeling bored. To my way of thinking, a thumb is more convenient than a pacifier because you don't have to worry about a thumb falling on the floor. But I have no objection to a pacifier if your baby prefers it, as some do. (Use only *safe* one-piece pacifiers—*never* tie a pacifier

144

to any part of a baby or crib because of the risk of strangulation.)

Either a thumb or pacifier is better for a baby than propping a bottle—which is an absolute no-no because the baby could choke—or letting a baby old enough to hold one go to sleep sucking on a bottle. Going to bed with a bottle results in nursing bottle cavities, which lead to early and severe tooth decay.

Thumb-Sucking in Older Children

Most parents don't mind seeing a baby suck the thumb but get a little up tight watching an older child do it. When they see their three-year-old sucking away, parents often feel they are somehow failing in their job. If Tommy were secure and happy with us as parents, would he need to do such a baby-like thing?

Parents do not have it in their power to make a child stop sucking its thumb. Nobody recommends coercive measures like the old-fashioned elbow splints once in vogue.

What you *can* do is remember that each child develops at his at her own pace. Development itself solves many parenting problems. As the child matures, he or she is better able to stop a "bad" habit. Also, parents *can* facilitate change in a motivated child.

The so-called tensional outlets, of which thumb-sucking is only one, increase during the preschool years. It's rare to see a four-year-old who doesn't suck the thumb or chew fingernails or stammer or fidget in some way.

Preschoolers are very busy at their job, which is learning about and organizing their world. A great many things are going on in their lives and things are changing every day. Growing up is a stressful job and children need some harmless release of tension.

Viewing the thumb-sucking habit as a harmless release of tension should help you lower your worry level. You can be absolutely confident that the child will outgrow the habit and, further, feel confident that you are not doing anything wrong in your parenting to cause this habit. In a sense, thumb-sucking in a preschooler is a sign of maturing behavior because the child seeks self-relief from tension rather than going to the parent.

Parents need not, and should not, do anything to interfere. But many parents need some help in carrying out a non-interference policy. I know I did. When I was feeling OK I ignored the habit, but when I was tired or cross the sight of my daughter sucking her fingers (she preferred the middle two fingers to the thumb) irritated me because I felt like a failure as a parent. If I was doing a good job how could my daughter possibly be tired or unhappy? On more than one occasion I lost my cool and told her to stop sucking her fingers and then felt guilty about saying it. She gave up sucking her fingers at about age five, when she was ready, but I regret the mixed messages I gave her.

Here's a suggestion I wish I had thought of then. Try putting a rubber band on **your** wrist and snap it to remind **you** that thumb-sucking is a harmless habit and you should not interfere.

After age five or so chronic thumb-sucking *can* affect the alignment of the child's teeth. But dentists themselves agree that thumb-sucking won't do any permanent damage to the teeth unless it continues beyond age five. If you are worried, take your child to the dentist. If the dentist says that the child's bite is not affected, everyone can relax. If the teeth are affected the dentist will advise you.

Some preschoolers who are slow in development or emotionally disturbed are constant thumb-suckers and, of course, these children need professional attention. A professor of pediatrics once said, "Thumb-sucking is nothing to worry about unless the child refuses to remove the thumb when the real thing is offered!"

Thumb-sucking in the older child? School-age children and older preschoolers may become embarrassed by their thumb-sucking because other children tease them and call them babies. If a child four or older asks for help in stopping thumb-sucking there are several things you can try.

Guidelines For Dealing With Thumb-Sucking In The Older Child:

- Don't nag, punish, yell, or name-call ("You big baby!").

- Make up your mind that the *child* owns the problem. The child is the only one who can stop the thumb-sucking. Your only job is to help motivate the child.

- Try to figure out if the child *wants* to stop sucking the thumb. Sometimes the child will tell you. Sometimes the child will be unhappy because of being teased by other children about this "babyish" habit. You can always ask.

- If the child wants to stop, you can try what the psychologists call "aversive taste therapy." Put a bitter substance on the thumb to remind the child to keep the thumb out of the mouth (products available in drug stores). I have seen this work well for motivated thumb-suckers or nail-biters over the age of five. (I do not recommend this for younger children or those who are not yet trying to stop their habit.)

- You can also try "paradoxical therapy" with the older child. Say to a child over five who starts to suck the thumb, "I realize you have a need to suck your thumb so I'll help you catch up on your thumb-sucking. You go to that chair and sit there and suck your thumb until I tell you to stop." This gets pretty boring and some kids, who realize they will be sent to a thumb-sucking place with nothing to do but suck the thumb, won't let you catch them at it too many times.

- Read a book called *David Decides About Thumbsucking* by Susan Heitler. (You can order the book from the publisher: Reading Matters, P.O. Box 300309, Denver, CO 80203, 303/757-3506, for $13.95 plus $3 for postage and handling.) The very title of the book reinforces the point that the child is the one who has to decide. The book starts off with a story, accompanied by wonderful photographs, about how a little boy named David learns to keep his thumb out of his mouth. Children who are concerned about their thumb-sucking will enjoy having their parents read this to them. The second section of the book teaches parents all about thumb-sucking and behavioral modification techniques that can help a motivated child stop.

- Limit TV and substitute more active things to do. Encourage the child to play out of doors, help the child start projects like collecting and labeling rocks to keep busy.

- Reassure the child that eventually he or she will be able to stop. Sometimes school-age children are able to keep their thumbs out of their mouths when at school or otherwise in public. But when they are at home, often while watching TV or at bedtime, they may still suck that thumb. This is common and, if the teeth are not affected, nothing to worry about, Eventually the habit stops.

Nail-Biting

ParenTips:

- *This Is the Most Common "Tensional Outlet."*

- *There Is a Genetic Component and an "Imitation Factor."*

- *Ignore and Do Nothing.*

- *Reduce Stress.*

- *If Motivated to Stop:*
  Try aversive taste substances.
  Use gold star chart.
  Try behavior modification—snap elastic instead.

Nail-biting is very common in children. Sixty percent of ten-year-olds bite their nails, which means that the non-nail-biter is in the minority at school.

Most children who bite their nails start doing this around age five but some start as early as age three or even two. Unlike most other mammals, we are designed so we can put our hands near our mouths all the time, whether we are lying down, standing, or sitting. It's easy to suck a thumb or bite a nail!

There may be a genetic component; nail-biting is more common among children whose parents were nail-biters and twins are likely to start biting their nails at the same time.

Children are also great imitators. If an adult in the household or family is a nail-biter, the child may think, "That looks like fun!" Thus, environmental as well as genetic factors play a role.

Perhaps the nail-biter starts by chewing on an already broken piece of nail or a nail that is rough and annoying. The child keeps on chewing because it is gratifying to chew away a problem all by yourself.

If you follow 100 children in the fifth grade who bite their nails some will stop, each year. Although nail-biting is pretty common in high school, by college age only 20 percent are still chewing their nails. By age thirty only 10 percent of the population are nail-biters.

Nail-biting is one of the so-called "tensional outlets." This term helped change our previous thinking that nail-biting and other such behaviors were bad habits. There is nothing "bad" about a child who chews his or her nails.

Tensional outlets like thumb-sucking, head-banging, and rocking are common in young preschoolers. Hand-to-face tensional outlets like nail-biting and nose-picking become very common in kindergarten, along with fidgeting behaviors.

All of us have bad moments when we feel tense and out-of-sorts. Indeed tension is universal. Adults have a repertoire of ways to relieve tension, ranging from "bad" things like smoking, to healthy things like taking a brisk walk. Children are more limited in their choices but have as much need to relieve tension as adults do.

Some parents think it strange that a child should feel tension. Isn't childhood an idyllic time with no worries? If a child has tension isn't it the parents' fault for not making the child's life smooth? The answer to both questions is "No." Childhood has its share of tensions; growing up is a hard job. Parents cannot, and should not, eliminate tension from their child's life. Every child has to learn ways of reducing tension that are socially and personally acceptable.

If a child is a nail-biter does this mean the child has an abnormal degree of tension? The answer again is "No". Years ago nail-biting was thought by the psychoanalytic school of therapists to be a form of self-mutilation. However, severely disturbed children who bite themselves to hurt themselves are very rare. Most childhood nail-gnawers do not hurt themselves.

Some children chew their nails only when they are under special stress like seeing a scary movie or taking a test at school. But in my experience most kids just bite their nails. The act of biting is a pretty unconscious one, which is why this is a hard habit to break.

The best thing parents can do about nail-biting is **nothing!** Nagging, reminding, scolding, ridiculing ("You look like a baby with your hand in your mouth all day long!"), or threatening ("You'll get an infection!" or "You'll have ugly hands!") are all useless. They may actually be counterproductive because the parental reaction makes the child even more tense.

Parents can observe the child to see whether there is a pattern to the nail-biting or if there is a particular time the child seems under stress. Parents can model ways of **reducing stress** by including the kids in exercise or "stress-breaks" when the whole family lies on the floor and does deep-breathing or imagines being in a peaceful place.

If the child is motivated and wants to stop nail-biting, you can try painting the nails with a **bitter substance** (products available in drug stores). My daughter saw a friend use this, asked for it, and it worked. It works because it makes the act conscious. The bitter taste tells the child that the finger is in the mouth so the child can take evasive action. Other helpful things include keeping the nails and cuticles smooth using emery boards and hand lotion.

You can also try the **gold star system.** Make a chart together. Let the child affix a gold star for every chew-free day. When a goodly number of such days accumulate—perhaps a week—there will be a special treat. It helps if the child selects the treat and the length of time.

Promising a manicure when the nails have grown in often works with little girls.

Whenever there is any problem involving your child's repeatedly doing one thing you want him or her to stop doing, I always like to suggest the *Child-Owns-the-Problem; Let-the-Child-Figure-Out-the-Solution Game.* In order for this game to work you need a verbal child aged five or older (although I've seen it work with some bright fours).

Have a "meeting" just like grown-ups do, preferably at a restaurant. Explain to your child that you want to have a talk. Ask your child about the nail-biting. Do you know why you do it? Does it bother you? Do you want to stop? If the answer to all three questions is "No," the child doesn't want to play and the game is over.

If the child does want to stop, **you stop talking.** Ask the child, "Jonah, you seem to have a problem with nail-biting. How do you suppose you might be able to fix it?" And wait for an answer. Sometimes the child can't think of an answer, sometimes the solution is magical or far too stern ("Tie up my hands in mittens.") but sometimes the answer is ingenious and worth trying.

However such a "meeting" is not always necessary. As problems in kids go, nail-biting is not a serious one. Accept the fact that this is the way your child relieves tension and that 90 percent of children who chew their nails stop by the time they are adults. This attitude will symbolize for your child your uncondi- tional love and acceptance as well avoid nagging.

Nose-Picking

- *This Is a Very Common Tensional Outlet of No Consequence.*

- *Don't Call Attention to the Behavior.*

- *QUIETLY Say "We Don't Do That in Public."*

- *If This Escalates After a Cold, Try a Humidifier.*

Nose-picking can really drive parents up the wall. The typical story: an otherwise pleasing child develops the habit of nose-picking, which is definitely not pleasing. The parents do not understand why the habit has started, are annoyed by the habit, and want it to stop.

Gesell (1977, page 256) pointed out years ago that tensional outlets, such as nail-biting and nose-picking, are most likely to occur when the child is under pressure. Pressure can come from one of two directions, external or internal. External pressure occurs when something the child cannot yet produce is demanded. Internal pressure happens when a child demands too much of himself or herself. In either case the solution to reducing the tension is to lighten up.

Boredom seems to increase tensional outlets as does waiting around for something to happen. TV is called entertainment but it often leads to *both* boredom and waiting around for something better to come on. Tensional outlets may peak during the child's viewing time.

How does a "bad habit" such as nose-picking get started? The hand-to-face movement that starts at birth is very common in children and continues in adulthood. We all touch our mouths or face at times. (Just now while I was thinking about what to write, my index finger left the keyboard and pressed my top lip.)

In some school-age children the hand-to-face movement results in nail-biting, lip-pulling, or hair-twisting; others may begin to pick their noses.

The first nose-pick no doubt occurs when the child is annoyed by the hardened or crusted contents of the nose and wishes to remove them. Unlike thumb-sucking, nose-picking requires a fair amount of hand coordination to be successful, so repetitive nose-picking is not seen much before age three or four.

Nose-picking continues because it works. This repetitive behavior relieves tension which reinforces the behavior.

Nose-picking is very common. It occurs in adults as well as children and in both sexes. Nose-picking is considered socially unacceptable in this and most, if not all, cultures. Everything that comes out of the body like the contents of the nose or bowel, spit, and menstrual blood are all considered unclean. The nose-picker is thought to exhibit lack of personal cleanliness and therefore is "disgusting."

Because all of us have noses which need cleaning I would venture to say that nose-picking may be universal, especially after a cold. However, older children and adults learn to do it in private or when they think no one is looking.

Though parents may be driven crazy by thumb-sucking or nail-biting in the school-age child, repetitive nose-picking is the least acceptable of all such behaviors and the behavior that parents most want to stop.

But young children have not yet learned social conventions so they pick away—and may even eat what they have gleaned—without realizing what the adults are fussing about.

Although such a behavior may start randomly, it might continue because of *parental* behavior. Scolding, nagging, shouting, and punishing not only fail to work but also seem to "fix" in place a behavior that might have just gone away by itself if parents had not called attention to it.

Parents do not have to put up with a behavior that they feel is repulsive. What do I suggest parents do with the child who repetitively picks at his or her nose?

- Don't call attention to the behavior.

- Focus your attention on the child, not the habit.

● When you see the behavior, get down to the child's level, look right at the child, lovingly put your hands on the child's shoulders and in a quiet voice say, "Josh, people don't like to see nose-picking. If you must pick your nose, do it in private."

This is very different from. "Josh, how many times do I have to tell you to get out of your nose. You've developed a filthy habit!" When you do it right, you are focusing on the child (not the habit), speaking to the child privately (not ridiculing the child in front of others), teaching the child that nose-picking is undesirable (without implying that the child is filthy), and giving the child a way of dealing with nose-picking in a grown-up way by going out of the room.

● You will probably have to remind your child many times before it "clicks," but each time focus on the child, not on the nose.

● Because crusted mucus in the nose is annoying, try to keep crusting at a minimum when the child has a cold. Humidifiers may help a little bit. You can also put a tiny amount of Vaseline on your pinky and gently rim the edge of each nostril.

We all have a responsibility to socialize our children so that they are acceptable to the society in which they live. The challenge is to do it in such a way as to promote self-esteem, which in itself relieves tension and in turn can diminish the need for tensional outlets.

Children's Fears and Worries

Separation and Stranger Anxiety

Fear of Doctors

"Preschooler" Fears

"Nobody Wants to Play with Me!"

Bullies

Parents' Fighting

Stranger and Separation Anxiety

ParenTips:

- ***Fear of Strangers***

  Normal behavior/indication of intelligence.

  Minimize by exposing baby to "new faces" from infancy.

  Leave baby with relative or sitter from three months on.

- ***Separation Anxiety***

  Also normal behavior.

  Will diminish as baby acquires awareness of object permanence.

  Never sneak out; always say bye-bye.

- ***Problem Separating At Preschool?***

  Be indulgent at first.

  After a few days leave quickly.

  Always say good-bye.

  Deal with your own guilt feelings.

  Rewards can work!

Stranger Anxiety

Just about every baby goes through at least a brief period of protesting when a stranger approaches. Stranger anxiety appears at about eight months, although some babies exhibit this as early as five months. Prior to about five months, Baby breaks into a grin of delight when *any* human face draws near. But with maturity comes a new realization: I don't know that face! Friend or foe?

This may seem to indicate that the baby is losing a sense of trust but the opposite is true. The baby is now able to discriminate among faces. Appropriately, the baby's behavior indicates trust of familiar persons but anxiety or caution at the sight of unfamiliar ones.

The baby's temperament largely determines the degree of protest. The placid baby may only squirm away so he or she no longer looks at the stranger's face. Shy babies may cry or even scream in fear. Most babies whimper a bit and turn away.

Needless to say, such behavior can cause tears in grandparents who were greeted with a smile when the baby was three months old, only to have the baby burst into tears when they approach a few weeks later. There can also be a problem when a sitter arrives.

Stranger anxiety is a **normal part of infant development.** However it may be that exposure to persons other than the parents from early infancy helps the baby get accustomed to other faces and minimizes manifestations of stranger anxiety.

I suggest leaving the baby with a relative or sitter once a week from about three months. If you wait until the baby is eight or nine months old you will be bringing sitter and baby together at the very time baby is at the peak of stranger anxiety. The baby **will** stop crying after you leave but this may be unnecessarily tough for the baby and it's definitely hard on the parents to leave a crying baby.

Separation Anxiety

Every child experiences separation anxiety in a natural and predictable progression.

Somewhere around six months of age the baby becomes smart enough to realize that the most important person in its life has left the scene, but is not quite smart enough to realize that you continue to exist when you're away. You'd be anxious too if you didn't know whether a loved one existed when out of your sight or if that person were ever coming back.

Children begin to develop a sense of object permanence somewhere around nine months of age. Now the baby realizes the ball that rolled under the sofa and Mommy who went into the kitchen both still exist. Parents help in the development of this maturity by leaving and returning to the scene many times so the child gradually learns Mommy and Daddy come back, by playing games like peek-a-boo, and by meeting the infant's needs so it develops a sense of trust that needs will be met.

But all this takes a while. Separation anxiety usually starts to diminish a bit at about eighteen months. By now object permanence is firmly established. Some children **know** Mommy is coming back but need a transitional object to tide them over until she does. (SEE PAGE 88)

Separation anxiety **can** persist in some children during all of the preschool years. However, most children by age three have the ability to think of a separation as temporary and have the capacity to "see" an internal picture of mother so it is not a major problem if she leaves. Strange settings like starting a new preschool may cause a temporary relapse. (By the way, boys are more likely than girls to experience separation anxiety.)

If separation anxiety persists beyond the early school years and is excessive, it is considered abnormal. Overanxious children may refuse to go to school, persistently worry that harm will come to their parents during the separation, and may even refuse to be alone. School refusal (phobia) needs treatment.

How does a parent handle separation anxiety in a preschooler? What should you do if your child cries when dropped off at school?

I believe in the *principle* of leaving the preschool reasonably quickly and quietly after dropping the child off. But **always** tell the child you are going to leave—never sneak out. Expect some crying and clinging at first but calmly bend down, hug the child, and say, "I'm leaving now. Mrs. Jones will take care of you until I come back. I love you. Good-bye."

There is evidence that children whose mothers make a **brief** statement ("I am leaving. I will be back soon. Have fun!") and **promptly leaves** do better than those whose mothers make a longer statement or prolongs the leave-taking. In order to profit from this knowledge, however, mothers have to deal with their guilt feelings. I know from personal experience how difficult it is to leave a crying child to go to work. But I also know that mothers who accept their status and deal with their feelings are helping their children as well as themselves.

A child who has never experienced separation from the mother may need special help at first. Sometimes you can arrange to stay at the preschool for the first day or two. But be sure you tell your child that this is not a permanent arrangement. "I will stay with you today (or today and tomorrow) until you get used to school, but then I will leave right after we get to school. The other children stay at school alone without their mothers and you will be able to do that too."

Not everybody agrees with me but I am a strong believer in the liberal use of rewards when a child has demonstrated desired behaviors. "If you let Mommy leave without making a fuss, I'll take you out for pizza after school." Do I worry that the child will expect special treats everyday? Not if the "bribery" is only used to get the child over the rough spots. In a few days nearly every child will not only tolerate but enjoy preschool.

Remember that some problems can be **prevented.** If babies have the opportunity to experience caretakers other than the parents from an early age, most will approach new people and places without an enormous fuss.

By age two a child should tolerate—without a fuss—being left at home with a sitter while the parents are out. By age three the child should be able to tolerate being left at a place other than home. These events may not always occur without protest but the protest is usually minor and short-lived. And, most important, such situations give the child the opportunity to practice adaptive skills.

Fear of
Doctors/Hospitalization

ParenTips:

- *Understand Why Your Child Is Afraid.*

- *Don't Be Embarassed by What Is Normal Behavior.*

- *Use Games and Role-Playing to Help Your Child Master the Fears.*

- *If Hospitalization Is Necessary:*
  Prepare child—but not too early.
  No surprises.
  No lies.
  Stay with your child.
  Empower child—play procedures on dolls.
  Expect regression.

All children go through a period of fearing doctors. Actually many go through **two** periods of doctor fear. The first is when the baby is dealing with stranger anxiety; the second is when the child realizes that the doctor represents a threat to bodily integrity—and to a child "invasion" of the mouth with a tongue depressor is just that.

There is a developmental sequence to childhood fears that parallels the child's cognitive development. A newborn fears not being held securely or falling as well as loud noises. (Someone once said the reason earthquakes are so frightening is that they evoke these two inborn fears of all humans.)

Somewhere between six months and nine months babies show fear of strangers because they have developed sufficient cognitive maturity to realize that the stranger is **not** Mother or Father. Doctors are very aware of this: the baby that gurgled and smiled at four months may scream at the nine-month check-up, not because the baby fears doctors but because all non-familiar faces are suspect.

Preschoolers know they are separate people and are developing their own autonomy. These wonderful accomplishments correlate with the child's concerns about hurting his or her body. To the child's way of thinking. the very sense of self is dependent on an intact body. If young children skin a knee, cut a finger, or notice a mosquito bite they may scream in terror, expressing a very primal fear that their body is about to disintegrate. Parents should understand this and provide Band-Aids even when they are not needed, as well as liberal doses of hugs and kisses.

It's easy to understand where fear of the doctor comes from in a three-year-old's mind. In the child's mind the doctor threatens the integrity of the body. The doctor always "invades" the child's body with an otoscope and sometimes with a needle.

Fear is the perception of a threat—real or imagined—and it takes a lot of maturity before a child can sort out real from imagined dangers.

How should parents handle their child's fear of the doctor?

Understand it. Accept the fact that it is a normal part of your child's development. Do not be embarrassed in front of the doctor or the office staff. They are used to it.

Reassure your children repeatedly that the doctor is helping them stay healthy and that you will stay during the examination. Don't say it's not going to hurt because if it does you will lose your credibility. "It only hurts for a minute."

Don't ever shame or demean children or say they are acting like babies. That will only make them feel less sure of themselves. Remind them that when they get bigger they won't be afraid of the doctor and that they are getting bigger every day.

Tell your child that when the exam is over you will do something nice together like get pizza or go to the zoo.

Help your child master the situation. Play with a doctor kit or play a game where first you, then the child, puts Band-Aids on Teddy Bear. Ask your doctor for a few tongue depressors and, after a few days, play a game of drawing pictures on them. I know one little boy who didn't want to touch the tongue depressors at first. But after the mother drew pictures he began to scribble on them and carried them around for several days as if to tell himself they didn't hurt.

There are times we *do* have to hold a child down in order to let the doctor complete the examination or let us take out a cactus spine or splinter. None of us like doing this but we have to put children's overall welfare above their feelings for a moment or two.

Fear of Hospitals

Doctors and parents both try to avoid surgery in preschool children whenever possible because hospitalization at this age can, in some instances, leave emotional "scars." In an emergency situation, surgery might be the only option. Life and limb must take priority. In the case of an elective (or, scheduled) operation, there may be a choice.

Ask the doctor why he or she is recommending surgery. What will happen if the surgery is postponed for a year or two? Will any permanent damage occur if surgery is postponed? What is the doctor's experience with children like this—how many get better on their own? What would the doctor do if it were his or her own child?

After asking these questions of Doctor Number One, get a second opinion.

Whenever possible, opt for ambulatory surgery so that the child does not have to stay in the hospital overnight.

The greatest fear that preschoolers have is loss of their parents or abandonment. This means that staying in a hospital would be scary even if nothing else were done.

Basic rules when hospitalization is necessary:

- No surprises. Prepare the child for what is about to happen.

- No lies. Don't tell the child it isn't going to hurt if it is.

- Stay with the child. Only admit your child to a hospital where parents can stay.

- Empower the child to master his or her fears.

- Empower yourself with knowledge about what is going to happen so you can best deal with your own fears. Act calm so your child will feel as calm as possible.

Do not start preparing the child too early. A three-year-old child should not be told that he or she is going to the hospital earlier than, say a day or two before the event. But you can "pre-prepare" the child by reading one of the many books designed to help children learn what to expect in the hospital.

I read *Curious George Goes to the Hospital* to my then four-year-old son several weeks before he was scheduled for surgery. We went back to that book on several occasions but also read lots of other books. I did not initially tell my son that this reading was to prepare him for his own hospitalization.

A day or so before he was scheduled to go to the hospital I told him that, like Curious George, he was going to the hospital. He had visited the hospital with me several times and knew what the place looked like. I told him what to expect and that I would stay with him. Of course he cried and said, "I don't want to go!" When his older sister looked in to see what all the fuss was about, he magnanimously told her she could go in his place!

Consider a pre-hospitalization visit. Most hospitals today encourage such a visit for young children.

Truth is critically important because children, especially those who are undergoing stress, must be able to trust their parents. Sometimes parents don't know what words to use. Nearly every child will ask: Will you be there with me? Will it hurt?

Tell the child you will be there right up until it is time to go into the room where the operation will be done. While the operation is being done you will stay right in the hospital waiting room, waiting for the operation to be over.

Tell your child what to expect: "We will go to the hospital at six in the morning. You can't eat breakfast or drink anything before the operation because that is the hospital rule. You will be put in a bed with rails but it's not a baby crib; even grown-ups have to stay in this kind of bed when they have an operation. You can take Teddy Bear and your Curious George book with you.

Tell children that they will not feel anything during the operation because they will be in a special, magic sleep. They will breathe into a magic mask and fall asleep. Do not say, "You will be put to sleep." because of the permanent connotations that phrase carries for pets.

Tell your child that there will be a special treat waiting at home because when people do something they don't want to do, a reward for good behavior is in order.

Ask children if they have any questions. Ask them to tell you what they imagine will happen. Some children worry that they will wake up while the operation is still going on. Children may think, somewhat correctly, that surgery is premeditated trauma arranged by their parents and doctor. Be sure to explain that the operation is not a punishment.

Empower children to conquer their fears. Encourage them to talk about and act out the operation on a toy animal. After the child comes home encourage talking about and acting out what happened.

Do not be upset if your child is clingy and tearful for a while after surgery. You may also see sleep and toilet training problems. This regression is normal.

"Preschooler" Fears

ParenTips:

- *Fears Are Normal, Healthy, Protective.*

- *Fears Do Not Indicate Future Cowardice, Emotional Problems.*

- *Big Three: Monsters, Thunder, Animals.*

- *Acknowledge Fears and Give Them a Name.*

- *Realistically Explain at Child's Level but Don't Try to Reason.*

- *Encourage Child to Talk About Fears.*

- *Give Child Ways to Master Fears (Visit a Calm Dog).*

- *Use Books about Fears, Monsters.*

- *Don't Be Embarassed!*

Parents are both surprised and troubled by the sudden, unexplained development of **fear** in their previously happy-go-lucky toddler. What turns a contented, imperturbable baby into a clinging or screaming toddler?

Maturity! The child is now old enough and smart enough to figure out that the world is not always a safe place.

All normal people experience fear or anxiety. Fear is the word we use when the object is identified—fear of a dog or thunder. Anxiety is that feeling we get when we feel helpless about the unknown or when we experience a vague, fearful feeling that we can't associate with anything.

Fear is not only normal, it is important to our survival. Fear alerts us to the presence of danger so we can protect ourselves. We want our children to have a healthy fear of realistic dangers like the automobile, but we don't want them to be so fearful that they won't cross a street.

The parent's role is to instill the importance of safety rules without making the child unduly fearful. The parent's task is to recognize that children's fears are largely universal (nearly all children go through a stage when they are afraid of animals, for example) and developmentally determined (children at a given age/stage experience similar fears).

It's important for parents to realize that fear is a feeling. All of us must feel free to experience and express our feelings because only through experiencing and expressing them can we deal with them.

Most important of all, parents must guard against their own concerns that the child's fear is abnormal, a sign of weakness is a bad thing—especially in boys, the fear will persist, or other people will think the parents' inadequate parenting has somehow caused their child to be fearful.

Fears in children, unless incapacitating, are **not** indicative of either an emotional problem or future cowardice.

When my son was about four he was terrified of bees. When he heard a buzz or saw a bee, this otherwise brave and outgoing little boy was reduced to a quivering, clinging child. I knew that my son had never been stung by a bee.

What did I do? All the wrong things! I tried to reason with him and explain the un-likelihood of being stung. I practically forced him to go out of doors to confront his fear. I told him big boys weren't supposed to act that way.

What should I have done? I should have allowed him to experience his fear and express his feelings without having to worry about getting me upset. I should have said, "I understand that you are afraid. When you get bigger you won't be afraid."

There are four basic mistakes parents make in dealing with their toddler's fears. **1)** Parents try to reason with their child. **2)** Parents force the child to confront the fear because they think facing the fear will make the child brave. Actually forcing the child to confront a fear before the child is old enough to deal with it can increase the fear. **3)** Parents punish or ridicule the child for having the fear or become angry so that the child tries to hide the fear. **4)** Parents ignore the child's fear or don't seem to be concerned or sympathetic. This makes children feel that their feelings are not valid or that their parents simply don't give a hoot about how they feel.

The big three of preschooler fears are **monsters, thunder** and **animals.**

Parents understand that monsters are scary and appreciate the fact that a loud clap of thunder can scare even a grown-up. Fear of animals is more puzzling. For example, a fear of dogs may come on suddenly and for no apparent reason. The child who previously said "Bow-wow!" and pointed to pictures or actual dogs with glee, suddenly reacts with terror when he or she spots a dog.

There is a reason. The child is now old enough to know that some animals can pose a threat but are still too young to distinguish which animals are actually threatening.

What can parents do to help preschoolers overcome and deal with their fears?

- Acknowledge the child's feelings and be sure to give them a name. I remember walking with my younger sister who would tighten her hand on mine when she spotted a dog far down the street long before she knew the words, "I am afraid." All the parent has to say is something like, "I understand you're afraid of the thunder. It's a real loud noise, isn't it?"

- Realistically explain what has to be explained. Even a young child can be told that loud noises don't hurt us and that thunder is caused by lightning. My father used to tell us that lightning was electrical energy that built up in storm clouds and that thunder was the noise caused by the air rushing into the space the lightning created. He taught us to count "One, one thousand…" between the flash of lightning and the clap of thunder to figure out how many seconds elapsed so we could estimate how far away the lightning was. He told us these things when we were much too young to understand them, but that gave us a rational scheme to deal with these common natural phenomena. And he never tried to talk us out of our fears. As a matter of fact he would deliberately jump as we did in response to a large peal of thunder and we would all say, "That was a BIG one!"

- Stay calm yourself. It's permissible, even desirable, to say, "When I was little, I was afraid of thunder too!" Children are remarkably reassured by the dyad of parental calmness and parental recounting of their own childhood feelings.

- Encourage the child to talk about fears. Ask the child why he or she is frightened. "What do you think will happen?" "What can we do about it?"

- Give the child opportunities to master the fear without coercing the child into a confrontation the child is not ready for. In the case of the child's fears of dogs, you could take the child to the home of a friend who has a mature, calm dog. (Avoid puppies; yes, they are small but they are likely to jump and get in your child's face.) Don't even suggest the child approach the dog, just let the child become comfortable with a dog nearby. If the child is not comfortable, try again another day. Do not approach strange dogs you see in the street to show the child you are not afraid because **1)** you don't know how the dog will react and **2)** you don't want your child to get the idea that it's OK to approach strange animals.

- Give the child further opportunities to master fears by using books. Show the child picture books of dogs and other animals so that the child can learn to make discriminations between all the animals that have teeth and come to realize that many will not bite. You can also play games with stuffed animals.

- Reassure fearful toddlers. "When you are bigger, you won't feel frightened of dogs."

- Use "magic" (spray bottle with water) to get rid of monsters under the bed.

- Do not be ashamed, embarrassed, or worried about this common, developmentally-related behavior in your child. Accept the fact that all young children will exhibit fears, understand that your child will be able to deal with these fears with time and maturation, and do not fall into the trap of thinking that childhood fears are a sign that your child will grow up weak or a "sissy."

Actually when toddlers express fear they are giving us a clear message that they are using their developing brain very well. They have learned to recognize the concept of danger! As they mature and as we empower them with knowledge, they will be able to sort out realistic dangers from imagined ones. This process takes time.

"Nobody Wants to Play with Me!"

ParenTips:

- *The Child Owns the Problem, Not You.*

- *Don't Over-React or Get Too Involved.*
    Don't assume child is suffering.
    Let child know you understand.
    Recall, talk about similar incidents from own childhood.

- *Let Kids Settle Own Disputes.*

- *Expect Your Child to Figure Out What to Do.*

- *Help Your Child Become a "Popular" Child Who:*
    Pays attention to other children.
    Listens to other children's requests.
    Praises other children.
    Takes turns.
    Expresses self clearly.
    Shows affection.

- *Teach Child Skills of Reaching Out to Friends.*
    If you **Include** and **Accept** you get included and accepted.

What should a parent do when you hear the mournful cry, "Nobody likes me!" or "Nobody wants to play with me!"? How do you deal with this common worry that many children express?

All parents want their children to be happy. We pray that they will suffer a minimum of the inevitable hurts of childhood.

When we see our child hurt by other kids or when we worry about our child not having children to play with, we remember our own childhood disappointments. And sometimes we overreact.

No matter how hard parents try, they have no control over which playmates live in the neighborhood. Even if the parents pick a neighborhood with lots of kids, families move. And even if there are plenty of right-age, right-gender children around, the kids may not get along.

The Importance of Play

Play is very important to children because play equals learning. As play helps baby kittens become cats, play helps babies become adults. Species that need to learn a lot, like the higher primates and humans, play the most. Play is vital to the social learning which is necessary for survival in our complex world.

Interactive play with others is the way children become acculturated to their own society. Anthropologists need hours of observation, but for children learning about their culture is literally child's play!

The Stages of Friendship

As with most behaviors in childhood, the way children interact with friends is developmentally determined. Toddlers know that a playmate is physically present but do not appreciate that the playmate is a "psychological" entity, another child with another point of view. Between about three and seven, a friend is someone you are playing with at the moment.

Children come to think of a friend as someone who does things they like but, though they recognize that another child might think differently from them, they don't quite understand the reciprocity bit. Somewhere between age six and twelve children figure out that friendship means some give-and-take, although they may look at this as a way of making the friend do their bidding. "If you play Lego with me then I'll play catch with you."

Children are approaching adolescence before they define a friend as part of an ongoing relationship based on the coming together of two separate and different individuals who cooperate for the sake of the friendship.

Nearly all children have "best friends" and value such friendships to the point of excluding other children. Boys often form clubs and can seem cruel in their exclusionary policies, but these clubs teach about getting along in a group. Girls often have their own pattern of exclusivity: two girls play together seemingly for the purpose of excluding a third girl.

Children, like all of us, are attracted to other children similar to themselves. Preferred friends are usually are of the same age, gender, size, and levels of intelligence and physical maturity. But cross-gender and cross-age friendships exist and are good for children because it's a wonderful way for children to learn about diversity.

What Makes a Child Popular?

Why do some children make friends easily while others struggle with this task? Studies of school-age children have shown that "popular" children **paid attention to other children,** praised them, listened to their requests, could take turns, expressed themselves clearly, and showed affection. In other words, the child who includes and accepts, gets included and accepted.

Shy children, children who are younger than the kids they are playing with and "try too hard," and children who are small for their age often have trouble with this business of including and accepting.

Popular children are not wimps, but they are not mean either. They know how to be both generous and assertive—they understand that others have needs and wishes but that their own needs and wishes are also worthy.

Friends You Don't Approve Of

It's a lot easier to say to a parent, "Let your kids pick their own friends—your children have picked up all your positive values and will soon drop their unsavory friends" than it is for the parents to do it!

There is some evidence that teens who are trusted to make wise choices usually do, while those whose parents are heavy-handed often continue on a path they know gets parental disapproval just to have something to rebel about.

You don't approve of a friend? It is OK to say that because a given child's behavior is unacceptable the child is not welcome at your home. But keep dialogue open. Ask your child why he or she likes this particular friend and explain why you object to the friend's behaviors.

The Parent's Role

Parents can play with their children but they can't play **for** them. The older the child is, the less the parents should become involved with the child's interactions with others. The more parents assume the role of "play police," the fewer incentives there are for children to work things out by themselves.

Obviously parents must see that their child is physically **safe** at play and suffers no lasting emotional harm from interactions with other children. But, because the child must figure out how to get along with others, parents should keep "interference" to a minimum.

My suggestions for parents who wonder how much they should get involved in their children's play situations and friendships:

- Don't over-react; don't automatically assume your child is suffering.

- Always let your child know you understand how he or she feels.

- Don't jump in to solve the child's problem. Whenever possible let children settle their own disputes.

- Only interfere to prevent damage to persons or property.

- Let your children know you expect them to solve spats and figure out how to get along.

- Ask the child—or the children if they both come to you at the same time— "What do you think you can do to solve the problem?"

- Unless you are dealing with a bully who must be stopped, try to avoid complaining to other parents about how their child treats your child.

- If yours is the youngest or a vulnerable child who always gets picked on, be creative. Think of places you can take your child to play happily—a community sports activity or a play group with children of the same age.

Bullies

ParenTips:

- *Bullies Can Be Stopped!*

- *Teach Your Child to TELL AUTHORITIES.*

- *Explain a Child's Right/Responsibility to Tell.*

- *Teach Your Children How to Avoid Looking or Acting Vulnerable.*

- *Help Children Develop a Sense of Personal Courage While Recognizing the Dangers of Today's Mean Streets.*

- *Work with School and Other Parents.*

- *Prevent Your Own Child from Becoming a Bully.*

- *Teach All Children Social Skills, Empathy, and Goodwill.*

- *Minimize Your Child's Exposure to Violence.*

Bullying is a fairly common problem. A recent study showed that one child out of seven is either a bully or the victim of a bully.

What is a bully? He or she is an overbearing person who habitually badgers and intimidates smaller, weaker persons using physical or verbal means. Bullies are different from other kids because they think bullying is fun.

Some say bullies have low self-esteem and feel so unsure of themselves that they only feel good when they are manipulating and controlling someone else. In other words they enjoy and seek out a sense of power. Others say that bullies lack social skills to influence others so they bully instead. But a major factor seems to be that bullies are themselves bullied. Usually bullies have been raised in families where spanking is used and combativeness is encouraged. They are subject to physical punishment and are not treated with respect by their parents so they get the message that it's OK to treat others the same way.

Which children are bullied? Three factors seem to be involved: gender, size, and vulnerability. Bullies and their victims are nearly always males. Victims are almost always smaller than the bullies, and victims project an air of vulnerability. Bullies are very good at sensing which child will show weakness.

Helping Victims

What can parents do if their child is being victimized by a bully?

- Always listen sympathetically to your children if they complain about a bigger kid who's harassing them. And pay attention to body language. If a boy seems subdued or worried or down, ask him if someone at school or in the neighborhood is bothering him.

- Teach your child that it is his right—and his responsibility—to go to the authorities. Any time he is terrorized by one or more bullies at school he should tell the teacher at once—and also tell his parents. If it happens away from school he should tell his parents.

- There is nothing wrong with telling someone in authority about bullying. "Tattling" is not a sin. In a democracy everyone should not only have an equal opportunity but also an equal right to be free from inflicted terror. Telling someone in authority helps protect other weak or small citizens of the schoolyard. Telling is **brave** because it helps make the school and streets safe for everyone.

- Tell your child that if he is picked on he should not feel he is doing anything wrong or that he deserves this fate. *The bully is the wrong-doer!* The child who is bullied should be helped to stand up for his rights. Sometimes the simple act of saying, "Stop bothering me!" takes the bully by surprise and he lets up.

- Help your child avoid looking or acting vulnerable. Teach the child how to look people in the eye, how to smile with friendliness and assurance, and how to walk as though he has a right to be on that sidewalk—which, of course, he has.

- Help your child develop a sense of personal courage. Self-defense lessons may be in order but your child should know he is taking these lessons to learn to defend himself, not to learn how to karate chop somebody. Although I don't believe in solving problems by physical means, sometimes it is appropriate for a boy to fight back. That usually takes the wind out of the bully's sails because he only wants to pick on vulnerable kids.

- Be sure your child understands the dangers of the contemporary streets. Some kids may have guns or knives, and the only appropriate response is to run away fast and tell someone in authority.

- If as a parent you see or hear about bullying in your neighborhood, whether or not your child is being bullied, *take action!* You can tell the bully to stop, you can tell his parents that their child's behavior is unacceptable.

Bullying Behavior Can Be Stopped!

The best defense against bullying is a child who tells the authorities and an adult who says that this behavior will not be tolerated.

Our culture expects boys to fight and to work out problems on their own. Our culture rewards bravery and looks down on telling the authorities because we prize individualism. But little bullies grow up to be big bullies—and raise their kids to be bullies. We don't need more violence in American society.

We now know that bullying behavior can be stopped. A Scandinavian project to stamp out school-yard bullying worked. (Bjorklund, David and Bjorklund, Barbara. "Battling the School Yard Bully." *Parents,* April, 1989.) Adults did not tolerate or permit bullying and intervened when such behavior was seen. Children were encouraged to report all violence and bullying. Parents of bullies were called to the school and helped to work along with the teachers to change their child's method of influencing others. Counseling was recommended when indicated.

If schools are to be successful in stopping bullying ALL children, not just victims, must be involved. Children who ignore bullying or stand by while their classmates are being bullied must learn how to support the victims and report the bullies. How? Role-playing both at home and in class is a start so all children know what bullying is and what to do about it is a good start. Rewarding supportive children who report for their courage and helping bullies find non-violent ways to interact also help.

Preventing Your Own Child from Becoming a Bully

How do parents prevent bullying or violent behavior in their own children?

- Give your children lots of **time and hugs.** Children need two parents and the knowledge that they are more important to their parents than anything else in the world.

- Because children learn how to act from their parents, **do not treat your children violently.** Don't spank. Never let your child see you act violently with each other, with a driver who cuts you off, or with an annoying person or someone who disagrees with you. Learn and model for your children non-violent ways of resolving conflict.

- Do not model, encourage, praise, reward, incite, or tolerate violence in any of your children.

- Teach your child how to handle anger—without hurting people or property—by pounding pillows or shouting in the shower.

- Limit exposure to our culture of violence. Control which and how many TV programs, video/computer games, and Internet sites your child can watch or use.

- Help your child grow up knowing appropriate ways to influence other children by teaching them social skills, empathy, and good will. Sometimes little kids have to be taught to smile when they walk up to another child. Sometimes bigger kids have to be taught how to make eye contact and talk in a pleasant and friendly way.

Parents' Fighting

ParenTips:

- *Learn to Fight Right.*

- *Before You Explode or Drop, Stop!*

- *Learn to Skirt Away from the "Edge!"*

- *Learn Negotiating Skills.*

- *Get Counseling If You're Not Fighting "Right."*

I don't think I've ever met a couple who didn't spat—at least once in a while. No matter how much love you have for each other there will be times when your wants simply do not coincide.

But children are happiest in a peaceful home because children love both their parents. Even a young child has empathy. If Mommy cries because Daddy yells, the child feels sad and may try to help Mommy or intervene. Children also may feel the conflict is their fault—-and often the argument IS about the children.

One school of thought holds that parents should never allow the kids to see or hear any marital discord. Talk about impossible goals! But even if parents *could* shield all their negative feelings and appear to agree all the time, they would be presenting a totally unrealistic view of marriage. Better that parents model for their children successful resolutions of the inevitable disagreements.

Why do parents fight? Parents are humans and all humans get angry and frustrated. The trick to becoming a grown-up is to learn how to handle anger and frustration. I, alas, took more years to learn this lesson than I would have liked, so I must confess my own children heard some shouting matches.

Some marriages are deeply troubled and fighting is a symptom not the cause. But often quarreling occurs in otherwise "good" marriages because of thwarted or unrealistic expectations.

Many of us go into marriage with unrealistic expectations of the degree to which our partner can help us when we are feeling bad. Every one of us will have a bad day when we are blue or tired and/or everything has gone wrong. No partner can "make it better." A partner may empathize with our feelings or offer to feed the baby but does not have the power to make us feel good instead of bad. Yet we want magic; we want someone to make it better. Also when we feel bad sometimes we project those feelings on a partner, which may lead to a fight but won't make us feel any better.

Really heavy stuff shouldn't be discussed or fought over in front of the children —or in front of anyone else for that matter. A public place is not the appropriate setting for private matters.

But the occasional bickering about whose turn it is to take out the garbage won't hurt the children. If the kids do see you fighting, then they should also see you kiss and make up afterwards!

Sometimes the fact the children are around helps keep parents under control so the argument doesn't escalate. One couple I know got help and changed their conflict-resolution style because their three-year-old threw up every time they yelled at each other!

For myself, I learned that I was more likely to be argumentative (which meant there was more likely to be an argument) when I was tired or frustrated. If I took a "time-out" so I could figure out what was really bothering me, I could often reduce the tension I was feeling and prevent a spat.

It's best to use "I" messages—"I hate to see the trash piling up!" —rather than "You never" (or "You always") messages—"You never take the garbage out until it falls all over the kitchen!" If there is a recurrent trigger, like the piled-up garbage, sit down together, this time *in front* of the children, and resolve the issue once and for all. Let the kids see how grown-ups can, without fighting, figure out how to solve a problem. Maybe the solution is as simple as a bigger trash can for the kitchen.

No Noisy Fights!

Parental fights are terrifying to children. Parents should **not** scream, throw things, or use physical violence in front of the children.

Young children are frightened by the noise of screaming. Seeing parents out of control is scary because children have trouble with their own impulses and depend on the external control provided by their parents. Further, children hate to see a parent hurt and every opponent in a screaming fight gets hurt.

If bickering and arguing become a way of life in your house, it's time to get professional help. Fighting simply takes too much human energy and generates too many unpleasant feelings to be tolerated. If you sprained your ankle, you would go to the doctor. Fighting all the time is a symptom of a sprained marriage that marriage counseling can often fix.

I use five "C" words to remind parents about what is needed for them to grow and develop as parents. The same words can be used to help parents understand what is needed in marriage.

First of all you have to **Care** about each other and you have to have **Commitment** to each other. You each need **Confidence** in your ability to make the relationship work, which means you need confidence in yourself as a person. You need to develop and nourish **Communication.** And finally, if you are ever "stuck" in the relationship and can't change unpleasant or destructive interactions, get **Counseling.**

A marriage that works, that nourishes each person, and allows each person to grow is a treasure. To live in the home that houses such a marriage is the best gift you can give your children.

What can I suggest for parents who have fallen into the habit of fighting, for whatever reason?

- Each partner should memorize and take to heart my little slogan, "Before You Explode or Drop, **STOP!**" Most fights start because somebody is close to the brink of exploding. You are hot or tired or over-committed or all three. You feel you are about to explode. Maybe you could hide your feelings if your boss walked into the room, but your spouse? Forget it!

- The key to **stopping**—whether you're about to start fighting with your spouse or screaming at the children—is self-awareness. Learn what it feels like when you are at the brink.

- Learn tricks to keep you away from the edge. The old adage about counting to ten still works. Also try two-minute "mini-breaks." Excuse yourself, go into the bathroom or your room, take deep breaths or image yourself in a peaceful place until you don't feel like exploding.

- Pick your battles and pick the place and time for them. Every couple learns to overlook the unimportant stuff. You also have to learn where and when to negotiate the big stuff.

- We don't have to act like cave men or women anymore. We are *born* with a physiological system that enables us to **fight** or **flee** when we are in danger or angry or attacked by someone else who is angry. But we can *learn* to **negotiate**. Fighting not only doesn't solve anything but it leaves both people feeling awful. Fleeing—or avoiding the issue—may prevent the fight but it doesn't solve anything either. The only thing that works is conflict resolution.

- Negotiating depends on each person's clearly—and quietly—stating his or her feelings; listening to the other person; and being able to compromise. When there's no screaming or name-calling it is not too difficult to learn how to negotiate.

- Fallout from fights is cumulative. In one sense the fact that we allow ourselves to "lose it" in front of a spouse shows we are secure in that person's love, but constant bickering and fighting can erode a relationship.

- If you and your spouse are in the habit of fighting and can't stop, get counseling.

Parents' Fears
and Worries

*"I Don't Spend Enough Time
with My Child!"*

"I'm Spoiling My Children!"

"My Child Must Do Well at School!"

"I Don't Spend Enough Time with My Child!"

ParenTips:

- *Provide Focused, Attentive Time.*
  You are **Close.**
  You are at the **Child's Level.**
  You are **Doing What Child Likes to Do** at the child's **Pace.**
  You are **Doing Nothing Else.**

- *Children Also Need to Have You Around (Being Present—But Not Interacting).*

- *Time You Spend with Your Children Should Be "CHILD-CENTERED TIME."*
  Developmentally appropriate.
  Your child likes the activity (shopping doesn't count!).

- *Do "Nothing" Together (like watching the stars).*

- *Avoid "Time Robbers."*

- *Be a Good Time Manager.*
  Be efficient.
  Plan ahead.
  Work backwards to plan your schedule.

Simplify your house and life.

Children need predictability in their life.

Decrease noise levels in house and car.

- ***Minimize Consumerism.***

  Everything you own means less time.

- ***Learn the Art of Doing More Than One Thing at a Time.***

  (a family hike = family time + exercise).

Every parent I know worries about spending enough time with the children. And every child seems to want more "parent time." A woman obstetrician told me that her five-year-old daughter keeps track of every delivery that takes Mommy away from home and expects "make-up" time!

The trouble is that everybody is busy these days—including the kids. It takes an understanding of the different kinds of parent-child time plus household strategic planning to pull it off, but, believe me, it can be done!

I have changed terminology—I don't use the term "quality time" anymore. I now call it "focused" or "attentive" time.

Why don't I use the old term when I give advice to parents? Because "quality time" cannot be defined and is a misleading expression. It became popular in the 70s when mothers began entering the work force in unprecedented numbers. Quality time became a rationale for some working mothers. When society questioned (which, of course, it always does!) whether they were neglecting their children, they could say, "I give my child quality time when I get home from work and it's the quality of time a mother spends with her children that counts, not the quantity."

The trouble is nobody really knew what quality time was nor how to measure it nor how much was needed.

Tom Boyce, a pediatrician and friend, wrote, "Quality time is simply a cultural myth." (Boyce, Thomas. "Life After Residency." American Journal of Diseases of Children, August, 1990). He went on to say that in his own experiences with his own children, "Moments of joy and extraordinary closeness do indeed happen, but they happen when they are least expected—utterly unplanned and unanticipated, in the most mundane and trivial of circumstances. The trick is to spend enough time with your children to allow these startling, rare, and unexpected gifts to arise—unannounced—out of the morass of day-to-day child rearing." Dr. Boyce was speaking to pediatricians, urging them to spend more time with their own children. He feels, as I do, that it is a myth that lack of time with children can be balanced with "quality" time.

There's another reason to spend as much time with your children as possible. **It's fun!** I am not sure the bleary-eyed parents of an eight-week-old with colic will believe me, but there are **joys of parenting.** There is joy in being needed, in being loved unconditionally by your child, in watching your child grow, in helping a totally helpless baby along the road to becoming a grown-up.

Of course the tasks of parenthood are onerous, especially in the early months. Of course the responsibility of parenting can be overwhelming. But don't spend so much time on the tasks or worry so about the responsibility that you lose sight of the little daily joys.

Focused Time

I know every child needs some focused time daily although I don't know exactly how much. But I am pretty sure parents can figure out how much their child needs by the very act of being attentive or focusing on the child.

Focused time is time when the parent is *doing nothing else* so that all of the parent's attention is focused on the child. You are in eye contact and/or holding the child so you two are *close.* You are at the *child's level,* both literally—on the floor—and figuratively—at the child's developmental level. You are *attentive to the child* so you can focus in on the cues the child gives you about what he or she needs at the moment. You are doing *what the child likes to do* and at the *child's pace.* Sometimes this is instructive time when you show the child how to do something.

Every child needs some of this focused time with each parent. No matter how many children there are in the family, each one needs some of this kind of time. No matter how busy Mother and Father are in their jobs, they must see that each child gets some focused time. Mothers who stay at home with their children shouldn't fool themselves. Even if you are there all day it may not be the same as **being there.**

There is no way that any parent can provide this high level of intense interaction all day long. Nor does a child want it or need it.

In her short story, "Quality Time" (in *Homeland*. New York: Harper.1989) Tucson author Barbara Kingsolver, wrote "Parenting is something that happens mostly while you're thinking of something else." And she's right. Children need and value another kind of time with their parents. I call this **present-but-not-interacting time.** This actually comprises most of the time we spend with our children.

You may be doing the laundry or working at your computer while the child plays in the same room. You talk to each other now and then but you aren't focusing on the child. You may take a break to go give the child a big hug or the child may look up and ask you, "Mommy, who made the world? At moments like this you shift from unfocused to focused time. These focused interactions may be brief but they are vital to the child.

Past research showed that working mothers demonstrate more of this intense interaction with their children than at-home mothers. I suspect these interactions are what we used to mean by "quality time". But in today's hectic world I find many well-meaning mothers who are on such a fast track themselves that they may actually be interacting too intensely. They are close and focused but moving and thinking at their own fast pace, not the child's. I try to teach working mothers the importance of quickly shifting to focused time and just as quickly slowing down!

Every child needs both present-but-not-interacting time and focused time. I never attempt to quantify the amounts for any mother, especially a working mother. She has to do this herself, taking cues from the child. She also has to learn how to adapt to the child's pace. Many working mothers tell me they feel better about their parenting after they master the art of focused attention and learn how to switch to this mode quickly. And I know the children benefit.

Child-Centered Time

Beware of the phrase, "I spend the entire weekend with my child!" Sometimes we fool ourselves into thinking because the child was along we fulfilled our "time requirement."

Kids can hate being dragged around the shops while parents do the weekend errands. Children need some of this so they can learn about the world and how we live in it. It helps to involve them in the planning (Which store shall we go to first?) and the shopping (While I get the meat can you get the cereal?). However, even shopping for something the child wants, does not generally fall into the focused-time category.

One couple I know who often eat late and prefer elegant dining frequently take their preschooler out to dinner. This child knows about sushi but often falls asleep at the table. Some of this could be a good learning experience but it is not child-centered time.

The most important criterion as in determining whether time is child-centered is that the activities you do together are **developmentally appropriate.** A toddler is not made to sit through long meals.

Another factor is whether the child likes the activity. By all means, if you are a tennis whiz, buy your child a racket. But if the child prefers soccer don't insist on tennis.

Special Time: Working Together, Hanging Out

One kind of "good" parent/child time is working together. Not only do the chores get done but you teach your child how to do the work and you **make the child feel valued.** When what we do is needed we feel good about ourselves.

Don't overlook that wonderful time of **doing nothing together.** Lie down on the patio some night and watch the stars together.

Be Efficient

Families today *are* stressed. In most households, both parents work. In most families the work day is lengthened by commuting time and the time it takes to drop the children off at child care and pick them up. Despite numerous "labor-saving" devices those managing a household must do the laundry, the dishes, the shopping, etc. and almost none of us has household help.

I have personal experience in raising children while working full time so I believe in **schedules.** I also believe in **planning ahead** and scheduling time for the inevitable contingencies.

I can offer harassed parents some ideas which either worked for me personally or have worked for other people I know.

Every Sunday night write out a day-by-day schedule for the whole week so everybody knows what to expect when. Post the schedule on the fridge or some other prominent place. Include the routine commitments (Pick up children at 6) and the unusual stuff (Sally-dentist appointment at 4). Don't forget upcoming events you will have to prepare for like Kate's birthday party and Tommy's camping trip.

When you are doing the schedule **always work backwards.** If you have to be at work at eight and it takes twenty minutes to get there after you drop off the children at school, you have to be at school by 7:35 in order to give yourself some leeway. And if it takes ten minutes to get to school, you have to leave the house at 7:20 because it takes a few minutes to unload the children. Being ahead of yourself brings peace of mind; being chronically late is a real stressor.

Take a long, hard look at what you do around the house and when you do it. Think about what chores or tasks can be **left out,** which ones can be **done less often** or less completely, what can be **done more efficiently,** and what you can **ask or pay someone else to do for you.**

Simplify your life and your household. If there are two preschoolers and two working parents in your family, this is not the time to get involved in activities outside the home. When the kids are older, you'll have more time for community or church activities. Right now give your children and the family priority. The more you simplify your lives, the slower the pace and the less stressed you will be. The less stress the parents experience, the less stress the children have.

Minimize the effects of the "morning rush". Make mornings as calm as possible by doing everything you can the night before. I used to lay out the clothes for the children (and myself) before I went to bed. The children and I routinely did the business stuff like permission slips for class trips, money for school lunches, etc. the night before. The children routinely put all the things they had to take to school like gym clothes and books in a set place so everything would be ready in the morning. Some parents make and refrigerate school lunches the night before.

Another suggestion that helps parents survive the mornings is to set the alarm earlier than you absolutely have to. Even if you are not a morning person, postponing the inevitable just makes it harder. Give yourself a few extra minutes to fully wake up or to enjoy a cup of coffee alone before you have to wake the kids.

Regular, nutritious meals at which the whole family sits down together are ideal. But, let's face it, such ideal meals are not always possible. Be a practical cook. Cereal, milk, and juice will meet the family's nutritional needs for breakfast. Don't even think about making pancakes or waffles until the weekend. And if everybody eats on his or her own while getting ready for the day, that's OK. Just be sure the children get up early enough to eat their breakfasts.

Children need **predictability**—especially young children. Let them know when the schedule changes and why.

Children don't need a bath every day—they need a bath when they are dirty. So if your toddler is very tired and reasonably clean, skip the bath and put the child to bed.

Both children and parents need to unwind after a busy day. And if you are fifteen-months-old, being in child care all day is a busy day. So have a **"Quiet Hour"** before bed. Read to the children, perhaps while the whole family lies down on the big bed together.

Stress is exacerbated by **noise.** Turn off the TV and stereo during the rush hour in the morning and when you are preparing supper.

Plan ahead so you don't run out of groceries or supplies. Running short means more trips to the market, which means more time on the road before everyone gets home. I bought things like toilet paper by the case. I always had at least two "emergency meals" in the cupboard or freezer. What's an emergency meal? The makings of an entire meal that you have on hand for the night you don't have time to go to the store. My favorite: a jar of spaghetti sauce, a box of pasta, a package of frozen vegetables, and a can of fruit.

Next to your schedule keep a blank **shopping list** made out in categories. The categories I used were dairy, meats, groceries, fruits, vegetables, paper, cleaning supplies, and drug store but you should make up your own according to the way you categorize things. Be sure everybody knows to write down "soap" when they unwrap the next-to-last bar.

Parents often pay so much attention to the children's needs that they ignore their own. Pay attention to yourself. Each parent should plan a **night off** from the family once a week while the other parent does double duty. (A single parent can trade off with another single parent.)

I know that money can be tight and that the way each of us spends money is very personal. But let me point out that help around the house like a cleaning service can be more valuable to the family than a piece of furniture. When my children were small I didn't have any furniture at all in the dining room but I had help in the house so I could spend time with the children.

Minimize Consumerism

It takes an enormous amount of time and effort to shop for and purchase and install or find a place for and maintain **everything!** The fewer things you have, the better off you will be.

What about all those appliances that are supposed to make life easier? All they do is clutter your kitchen counters and cabinets.

It took me years to learn that before every potential shopping trip I ask: **Do I really need this? Do I really want this? Will it make my life easier or harder?**

On the other hand, things that are used a lot or always needed should be purchased ahead. Examples. Paper napkins, birthday cards, wrapping paper, and "emergency" toys.

Doing Two Things at the Same Time

Take advantage of some ways to do two things at once. Family meals together provide both food and "togetherness." When driving the kids to school you can play word games. Take a family hike to provide both family time and exercise.

But don't try to write your novel and pay attention to your child at the same time—both literature and child will be short-changed!

Minimize Guilt

Guilt is an exhausting emotion. Do the best you can to meet your children's needs and your own needs. Hopefully, this ParenTip has suggested strategies to minimize time pressures in your houslehold. Maximize the positive effects: **Stop worrying!**

"I'm Spoiling My Children!"

ParenTips:

- *Spoiling Results from PARENTAL Behavior.*

- *Trust Me—a Spoiled Child is NOT HAPPY!*

- *Appreciate That Every Child Acts Spoiled Some of the Time.*

- *The Crying Infant, the Toddler Who Gets into Everything, and the Two-Year-Old Who Says "No!" to Everything are Not "Spoiled" Children; These Are Developmentally Normal Behaviors.*

- *Prevent Spoiling By:*
  Being in charge.
  Saying "no!" when appropriate.
  Striving for consistency.
  Limiting "stuff."
  Setting limits.

What is a spoiled child? Pediatrician Bruce McIntosh ("Spoiled Child Syndrome." *Pediatrics,* January, 1989.) defines the spoiled child syndrome as characterized by **self-centered and immature behavior resulting from the failure of parents to enforce consistent age-appropriate limits.**

Spoiled children are not considerate of others, always want their own way, cannot delay gratification. They are intrusive, obstructive, and manipulative.

They are difficult to satisfy and unpleasant to be around.

Penelope Leach (1989, page 467) says your child is **not** spoiled if you enjoy spending time with the child, if the child enjoys the time and things you provide, if the child can accept "No" most of the time, and if the child changes your mind by "reasoned or passionate argument," not by making a scene.

The important thing to remember about the spoiled child is that **the child is NOT happy.** No matter how many diverting possessions the child has, no matter how often the child gets his or her way, no matter how indulgent the parents, no matter how many times a day the parents give in to the child, the kid is miserable.

It is important to realize that **every child will act spoiled occasionally.** But the spoiled child has the obnoxious behavior patterns all or most of the time.

There are three age-specific normal behavior patterns that parents may think indicate spoiling but do not: the newborn infant who cries—even cries a lot—the toddler who gets into everything, and the two-year-old who says "No!" to everything. It's OK to pick up the crying infant, encourage safe-exploration by the toddler, and accept negativity in the two-year-old. These behaviors are all developmentally normal, although the way you act or react could prolong them all.

Some children exhibit spoiled behavior because they have another problem. Examples include the temperamentally difficult child and ADHD. Some children exhibit spoiled behavior because there is family stress like divorce or illness.

Several child behavior patterns that fall into the "spoiled child" category **are invariably caused by inappropriate parental behavior.** These include trained night feeding, trained night crying, and recurrent temper tantrums. All of these problems are best prevented by **appropriate parental behavior.**

Do not feed an infant every time it cries. Hold off a bit, cuddle and croon, use a swing or a pacifier until the baby is gradually able to tolerate longer intervals between feedings and night feedings will diminish. Do not let the baby fall asleep in your arms. Feed, change, cuddle, rock—but put the baby down when still awake (SEE PAGE 45). **Ignore temper tantrums** (SEE PAGE 106).

Prevent spoiling by being a parent who loves your child enough to:

- **Say "No!"**

- **Strive for consistency.**

● **Set limits.**

● **Understand and deal appropriately with your child's behavior.**

By the way, spoiling is not just a matter of over-indulgence. Ordinarily, parents cannot give their children too much time or attention (or even, to a degree, material "things") provided the parents also **provide clear expectations and set limits.** Indulgence leads to spoiling when a parent who lacks confidence, time, or energy (or all three together) tries to meet the child's needs with material gifts and fails to provide guidelines for acceptable behavior.

If you over-indulge and under-limit, your child will likely come down with a bad case of the "Gimme's." Better to teach your child to delay gratification and think of others.

"My Child Must Do Well at School!"

ParenTips:

- ***Read!***

  Read to your child and let your child see you read.

  Establish a family reading hour.

  Limit all screens: TV, computers, games.

- ***Teach Your Child the Three New "R's"—Respect, Responsibility, Reason.***

  Teach your child how to be responsible.

  Help your child learn how to reason.

- ***Respect Your Child, Model Respectful Behavior, Teach Your Child to Respect Others.***

- ***Be an Educated Parent about School and Learning.***

  Encourage and revere learning.

  Have high expectations.

  Learning is work; knowledge is fun.

- ***Be a Homework-Savvy Parent.***

  Provide equipment, environment for homework.

- ***Child Owns Homework; It's the Child's Responsiblity To:***

  Bring homework home.

Remember to do it.

Take homework seriously.

Remember to take it back to school.

- **Only Help If The Child Is Stuck.**

- **Encourage Child to Ask for Help.**

- **Help Child Recall—"What Did Your Teacher Say?"**

- **Show Child How to Look Things Up in Book, Dictionary, Encyclopedia.**

- **Give Child an Easier Example to Boost Confidence.**

- **Show Child How to Break Tasks Down into Doable Parts.**

- **Show Child How to Review Material and Self-Test.**

All parents want their child to succeed at school. Genetics plays a big role in school success as does the quality of the school, but parents can help in four areas: encouraging reading, teaching the three new "R's," working with your child's school, and being a homework-savvy parent.

Read!

Every parent knows it's important for parents to read to children.

Start early!

You can't make an Einstein out of your child by reading because genius is born not made. But children whose parents read to them, and who live in a house where there are plenty of books, do better in school than those who have not had these advantages.

Name every object **every time you use it.** "Here's the diaper!" "Look at the red ball!" "Look, Jenny! A real doggy!" Always verbalize safety rules: "Stove hot! Don't touch!"

Read with an **excited, animated** voice. Use lots of expression; ham it up!

Hopefully your baby will imitate your behavior and become enthusiastic about books later on. Don't ever sound bored even if you are reading the story for the thousandth time. I used to change the story a bit to amuse myself but when my children got to be about eighteen-months-old, they had memorized each book so well that they protested even my most creative variations.

How can parents help their children maintain enthusiasm for books and reading? **Read to your young child every day. Buy books** instead of junk toys at the supermarket. Make the visit to the **library** for Story Hour and a new supply of books a weekly treat. Give your child choices at the library so he or she decides what books will be read that week. Show your child how important reading is by reading signs out loud. "That sign says Santa Claus is to the left. Let's go!"

Don't feel you have to teach your child how to read before he or she starts school. However, you can encourage your preschooler to "read" to you from familiar picture books. Play a game in which you read one page and the child "reads" the next. The child will remember the words exactly or will at least tell you the gist of the story. The child will also have a fun opportunity to imitate the rhythm of your voice which is important to the development of reading aloud.

Be a Reading Role Model

Probably the best way to get a child in the habit of reading is to be a **reading role model.** Always have newspapers, magazines, and books in the house. Get books for yourself when the children get their books at the library.

Start a **Family Reading Hour** by setting aside a time when **everybody** reads. Turn off the TV and radio. First read something aloud; then let everybody read a book silently. A pre-reader can be given a pile of picture books and will usually enjoy imitating what everyone else is doing—turning pages. Keep the silent reading time short if your baby is too young to turn pages without getting bored.

When the children are old enough, rotate the person who reads aloud at the family reading hour so everyone gets to practice reading aloud—an art almost lost today. Always let the children help decide what book to read.

Reading goes with **writing.** Be sure your house has plenty of paper and crayons or pencils around and give your baby lots of opportunity to scribble. Pretend to write letters to Grandma. I have a note on my fridge which reads

"Dear Grandma, Adam says 'Thank-you' for the presents you sent and is learning to write his name." This is followed by some of the most extraordinary scribbles ever done by a two-year-old, one of which almost looks like an "A"!

Limit ALL Screens!

To foster a love of reading in your child, turn off the TV. Let me remind you that a TV set always comes with a switch that can be turned off. Use that switch! Don't let TV be a constant background to your family life. If you want your child to become an avid reader, be sure your entire household spends more time reading than watching TV.

Also, limit time in front of computer screens and video games. Some parents think they are helping their preschooler by showing the child how to use the computer and getting software that purportedly teaches a child how to read or spell. It's great to give children the advantages of a home computer if you can, but the skills of matching symbols on a screen are not the skills needed in reading. Children learn hand and eye skills but not how to read.

The best combination for success in learning how to read is the old triad: **baby, mommy's lap** and a **book**—all brought together frequently.

Don't let your school-age children spend all their spare time at video games or even educational computer programs. Success in our complex world depends on communication. Communication depends on reading plus interaction with others.

The Three New "R's"

We're all familiar with the old three "R's"— reading, writing, and 'rithmetic. There are three additional "r's" that all of us—parents, teachers, clergy—must teach our children: Respect, Responsibility, and Reason.

1. Respect

To my way of thinking we need an Eleventh Commandment: **Respect your children.** We all know we should honor our fathers and mothers. But sometimes parents have to be reminded that children as well as adults should be treated with respect.

Parents, of course, have the responsibility of socializing the child and at times we need to be dictatorial. ("You may not hit your baby sister!") But the skillful parent pays attention to the child's feelings and never criticizes the child—only the behavior.

If you want to teach your children to act respectful then model respectful behavior. If parents are courteous and respectful to each other and others, your children will act that way—at least most of the time.

Alas, modeling the behavior you want is not the whole story. We must also **teach** our children about respect, why it is important, and what skills are needed to be respectful. Respect, starts with *self-respect*. The child who feels good about himself or herself can empathize more easily with the feelings of others.

But empathy has to be taught, explained, and reinforced by the parents from an early age. "How would you feel if Sally took your doll?" "How would you feel if somebody called you a sissy?"

Parents must also teach children the concept of fairness. If there are two cookies, each child gets one. It is not fair for the bigger one to get two.

Children must also learn how to empathize with and be protective toward those who need our protection: the young, the elderly, "special" children.

Children have to be taught that people come in all colors, sizes, shapes. Every person has feelings and each of us deserves respect. We must not only tolerate diversity but embrace it as it strengthens us all.

The bottom line is that we are one people on a fragile planet.

Parents should begin talking about social issues when children are very young. We teach not only how to share but also why we share. We teach that it's wrong to hurt people; it's wrong to steal from people.

And don't forget about respect for things. "We don't write on library books because they belong to all of us." "We don't litter; if everybody did there would be no room to hike because the path would be full of garbage." "We don't pollute. Remember it's a fragile planet."

2. Responsibility

The second "R" stands for **Responsibility.** All of us have come across obnoxious kids who seem to think they that **1)** they are entitled to everything they may want and **2)** nothing they do is ever their fault—it's always the other guy, the teacher, etc.

Nobody is entitled; all of us have to earn our space on this planet. Nobody can put all the blame on others. Every adult must be responsible for his or her actions and behaviors. And children must learn about being responsible long before they become adults.

How do we teach responsibility? First of all, **start early.** Even toddlers can be expected to pick up toys and put clothes away. Chores are a vital part of family life. Wise parents give their children increasing levels of responsibility for chores.

Intuitively one might think that with all the employed parents out there, more children would be doing more chores. I hope this is true but some employed mothers I know do not involve their children in chores. Some feel guilty because they work and spend so much time away (I can well remember such feelings) but most, I suspect, are simply too tired. It's often easier to do something yourself than to teach the children how to do it.

Responsibility includes **self-discipline.** Children must learn to be responsible about homework, keeping appointments, planning schedules. A successful thirtysomething I know told his mother that she provided the basis of his success by teaching him self-discipline, starting with piano practice.

3. Reason

When I talk about the third "R", **Reason,** I am talking about the capacity for **rational thought, critical thinking** and **individual decision-making.**

Children today know lots of facts. We reward this knowledge at home. Schools reward the acquisition of facts. Children also need to know how to think, how to figure things out for themselves, and how to exercise good judgement.

But we can't wait until the child goes to school to begin teaching about how to think. Even though children do not have the capacity for abstract thought until about twelve, children should be given the opportunity to make concrete choices (a blue or a red shirt, an apple or a tangerine) when they are very young.

Later, both at school and at home, children need to think about and understand **cause and effect** and **what makes a good choice.** One day they must be able to figure things out for themselves and not make decisions based on what someone else thinks or what they hear on TV.

Children of today will be adults in the 21st century. Nobody can predict what their lives will be like but we can say with certainty they will experience many changes in the world. All they can expect with certainty is that *change will be the norm.* In order to cope with the world of their future, our children must learn how to think. We parents have a critical role in teaching our children how to think critically.

Ask questions at the dinner table ("What can you think of to help the home-less?").

Role-play as a family ("Jesse, let's pretend Daddy lost his job. How would you feel? What do you think we could do?").

Assign topics for each member of the family to look up and report on next week.

Start a family recycling project.

Take the children with you when you deliver food to the food bank.

Work with the child's school to be sure your child is learning how to think. The next century will be a competitive one. Cognitive knowledge and skills will be even more important than they are today.

By the time children finish school they should be able to think for themselves, express their thoughts both verbally and in writing, and be able to tolerate ambiguity, i.e., understand and accept the fact that there is seldom one answer.

Parents play an enormous role in modeling and teaching these "R's" to their children. Perhaps this is the most important task of parenting—imparting those values that give meaning to the term *human* beings.

Be an Educated Parent about School and Learning

Parents can't make their child a genius; only their genes can do that. But parents can and should model a love of learning, curiosity about the world we live in, and reverence for learning.

Have high expectations for your child. **Expect** both your sons and daughters to do well at school, find a productive and satisfying life's work, and become useful and concerned citizens. This is not just self-serving—our democratic way of life depends on an educated citizenry.

Parents like to make learning fun for their children. Those brightly colored, cleverly-designed educational toys work well for young children. However I suspect children have such a **need** to learn that unless parents get in the way they will learn even in black-and-white and—gasp!—even in the absence of educator-approved educational toys.

But there comes a time when there must be a paradigm shift. **Learning can be hard work, knowledge is fun!** I went to the recent opening of an exhibit designed to teach kids about pollution by automobiles. The dignitaries inaugurating this exhibit assured the audience that their goals were to make the exhibit informative and *fun*. I was turned off by the bouncing balls, bells and whistles—and I suspect older kids would feel the same way. Information itself should be considered the fun part.

Practically speaking, be sure your children understand that learning may indeed be work but the rewards are great. Knowledge gives us power and understanding and joy.

Homework

Parents play an important role in their child's education. It's simplistic and unwise to think that the teacher does it all.

All parents must take an interest in their child's schooling, know what material the child is covering in school, and be in communication with the child's teacher.

Parents should let the child see how they do "home" work. Show your children how you do things that require organization like paying bills. This teaches children how a necessary task is approached and carried out. You can also let the child help—licking the stamps makes the child part of the process.

What role parents should play in the child's homework is a bit of a dilemma. Sink-or-swim vs parental involvement?

There is no question that parents should not do the child's homework nor assume responsibility for getting it done. On the other hand I don't feel sink-or-swim is the way to go.

I firmly believe that there is a place for thoughtfully considered parental help. My philosophy of parental involvement in homework can be summed up in three principles.

Parents provide the homework environment. Children don't have the wherewithal to buy a desk or a dictionary. That's your job.

Every child needs a quiet place to work with no other people or distractions around. Ideally this is the child's own room. If the room is shared with a younger sibling, parents need to find a creative solution that will give the school child the proper environment for work without interruption.

Every child needs the necessary *equipment* for homework just as you need tools or equipment at your desk at work. To start, the child needs a desk or table with good lighting, an age-appropriate dictionary, paper, pencils, etc. Later parents may need to add a calculator or even a computer. Although you should always take the child with you when you shop for school supplies, *it's your job to see that the child's work space is set before the first day of homework.*

The child owns the responsibility for homework. This must be clear to everyone. It is the child's responsibility to:

- Bring homework home.

- Remember to do it.

- Take the work seriously.

- Remember to take it back to school.

Parents should be available to help if the child is stuck. And parents must know how to help **the right way.**

A child who is stuck can do several things: Figure it out. Look it up somewhere. Stare at the paper for hours. Give up. Ask for help.

A child in the early grades is limited in his or her ability to figure it out or look it up. If your child asks for help (and I would encourage your child to ask, certainly in the early years), give it.

There are several ways parents can help without doing the child's work:

- Help the child recall what he or she has learned. "What did the teacher tell you to do?"

- Show the child how to look something up—the dictionary or encyclopedia, or the math book for a sample problem.

- Give the child an easier example to boost his or her confidence level.

- Show the child how to break down the task into doable parts.

- Check the child's answers if the child seems worried about the work. If the answers are right, the child will feel confident about the work. If the answers are wrong you can point the child in the right direction.

- Encourage the "stuck" child to take a break for a few minutes.

- Be sure no child spends too much time on homework. If the child seems to be doing so, find out whether this is a "staring-at-the-paper" phenomenon or real homework overload. Overload can arise in two ways: the child needs extra help in order to keep up or do the work or the teacher assigns too much. Either way, talk to the teacher.

- Help your child make the transition to self-help. My daughter wanted me to test her on her spelling words before the weekly quiz. I showed her how to test herself by covering up each word, writing it down, and checking if what she wrote was correct. I gave her a red pencil so she could play teacher as well as pupil. She was proud she could do it herself and no longer needed my help.

- As long as parents do not do the child's homework or take over responsibility for it, judicious parental help can make a big difference both in the child's skills development and attitude toward schooling. Saying, "Ask your teacher," or "I'm too busy," or "It's your problem." could give a message that you are not interested in your child's success at school. I can't think of a worse message.

Comtemporary Parenting Problems

Teaching Children Values

Toys: Less Is More

Limit TV, Video Games, Computers

Painful Realities/Difficult Situations

Manners

Chores

Money

Teaching Children Values

ParenTips:

- *Be a Good Person.*

- *Model Ethical Behavior.*

- *Teach Your Children about Values; Use Examples from Daily Life to Push Your "Parent Propaganda."*

What is a "value" anyway? Values are standards of actions and attitudes that shape who we are, how we live, and how we treat others.

A value increases as it is given away in the sense that the more given to others the more we get in return. Beauty or genius is not a value because it does not increase as it is given away.

Values make society livable and workable. Our job as parents is to pass them on to our children. Individual and collective happiness and well-being are connected to behavior that is governed by moral values. Children might learn on their own that if people lie they won't be trusted, but we don't have time to learn such things on a trial-and-error basis.

Just as children reared in a reading home become readers, children reared in a moral home become "good" people concerned about others. **Parents must be good, model good behavior,** and **talk/teach** about good behavior. It takes a long time to rear a moral person. Parents should start early; don't wait for Sunday School.

There are specific values that we as parents must teach. For example **honesty** is important in a complex society. We teach about honesty by setting an example and rewarding honesty. We also provide a safe environment for our children to express themselves and "try out" truths and lies. We understand that developmentally based preschool fantasies ("The dog did it!") are not really lies (SEE PAGE 125). We explain "white lies" and use them in order to avoid hurting others. We play truth games with young children ("The sky is green!" is false) and discuss truth dilemmas we have experienced with older children.

We must specifically teach about other values like **caring for others** (teach the Golden Rule), **tolerance** (teach that diversity is healthy and ambiguity can be tolerated by thinking people), **courage** (dare to not follow the crowd), **peacefulness** (understand another's point of view and control your temper), **kindness** (best taught by example).

To my way of thinking, three very important values are **respect, responsibility** and **reason.** (SEE PAGE 196)

The most valuable thing I can say to parents about values is **stand by your own values** no matter what the world is doing.

Our children live in a world that emphasizes sex, violence, instant gratification, and consumerism. As parents we **encourage** our children to be independent of us and make choices for themselves.

We ask a preschooler, "What color tee do you want to wear?" without dreaming how to respond when a daughter wants to choose to wear makeup at ten!

It bothers me that all the people giving parents advice—including me—have not been smart enough to sound an alarm. We have not figured out a way to help parents both encourage autonomy, which is healthy, and keep their kids from growing up too fast, which is not.

Parents must learn to say no without feeling bad when no is the right answer. When a child asks for something that is totally beyond your means, it's OK to refuse to buy it.

Of course you hate to disappoint your children. Parents have always dreamt of indulging their children, gratifying each child's wishes, and somehow making the child's childhood idyllic.

Today, parents seem more anxious than ever before to give their children what they ask for. And parents often experience anxiety if they are unable to fulfill their child's desires. They feel this will in some way harm the child.

Why are parents—even those who can ill afford it—so into kiddie indulgence today? Perhaps some parents remember their own childhood disappointments and want to prevent similar disappointments. Perhaps some parents are trying to keep up with those Jones parents who provide their kids with designer sneakers and jeans.

Maybe some parents think that they can substitute **things** for **time and attention.** I well remember feeling guilty because I spent so much time at work away from my children.

Things are not time. And **indulgence** is not healthy for children because it retards the development of a own sense of responsibility.

The child who gets everything he or she asks for views the world as a place where *other people provide gratification.* That's exactly right if we're talking about breast-feeding, but after infancy we have to learn that we are responsible to provide our own gratification by working for it.

How does a parent say, "No, you can't have that?" Firmly, quietly, in private whenever possible, and without guilt. There's nothing shameful or selfish about being on a budget and spending your hard-earned money wisely.

Parents must get in touch with their own feelings first in order for this to work. Shake off any guilty feelings. You're not a mean Mom, just a realistic one who knows what her budget can provide. Also, you can get together with other parents who share your values and agree that nobody on your block gets $200 athletic shoes!

You are **not harming** your children. As a matter of fact you are teaching them important lessons about life's realities.

Toys: Less Is More

ParenTips:

- *Avoid Toy Overload!*

- *Buy "Nutritious" Toys and Limit "Junk" Toys.*

- *Consider Child's Age, Skills and Interests Before You Buy.*

- *Teach Children How to Avoid Toy Confusion by Putting Toys Away.*

- *Teach Children How to Share.*

- *If Toy Guns Make You Uncomfortable, Ban Them from Your House.*

What is one of the most common and preventable problems of contemporary childhood? **Toy overload!** Today's kids have too many **things!**

I have nightmares of children drowning in a sea of brightly colored plastic objects while their parents and grandparents rain even more toys down on them. The poor kids don't have room to move around in this confusion of toys, let alone find the toy they want. And, what's more horrifying in my vision, is that the kids keep asking for more toys because they can't find anything to play with.

The other night I felt irritated because I couldn't find anything to wear. Fortunately I have learned through the years that this means it's time to clean out the closet and give away un-needed stuff—not time to go shopping. But children don't have the capacity to deal with toy overload, so parents have to think through carefully what symptoms toy overload can cause and how to avoid this problem in their own household.

Play is vital to all young mammals because play equals learning. Species that need to learn a lot, like higher primates and humans, play the most. One of the most important tasks of parenting is to provide an age-appropriate milieu for play.

Play with objects like toys is an important kind of play and fills an important developmental need. Play with objects helps children find out what things are and how they are used. Children imitate the way adults use objects. Children also use objects to express themselves and to have social interaction with other children.

So every child needs *some* toys. The question is how many and what kind.

I can't fault parents for wanting to make their children happy on birthdays or Christmas but I urge caution and restraint.

Parents and children are literally bombarded with commercials for what I call "junk toys". These are usually plastic, breakable, un-repairable, anti-imagination (the child can only do one thing with them), widely-advertised and widely-displayed toys. They often come in a series so children want the whole set.

Children today often feel "entitled" to get whatever they see advertised. Affluent parents may think, "Why not, we can afford it." Struggling parents may feel sorry for their children because they don't have year-round advantages, so they overbuy at Christmas. Working parents may think—consciously or subconsciously—that toys substitute for time. And all of us parents may cave in to the kids' demands just because it's too darn difficult to resist.

Suggestions to help parents resist temptation:

- Avoid junk toys.

- **Do not buy too many toys!** My grandson tore off wrappings one birthday in what looked like a feeding frenzy. He rushed from toy to toy without savoring anything. Better one present from Mom and Dad and one from Grandma and Grandpa that can be appreciated.

- Buy developmentally-appropriate toys.

- When buying toys, consider the child's skills and talents and what he or she likes to do.

- Concentrate on "nutritious" toys. These toys are sturdy, can be used over and over again, and can be used in several different ways depending on where the child's imagination goes that day. Nutritious toys are building toys like Lego; items that foster creativity like crayons, paint sets, and clay; sports equipment; and objects that imitate what adults use like trucks, dolls, and dishes.

- Remember that, although the toy belongs to the child, the child may need some parental input, especially with tough-to-figure-out directions. When play with an object starts to flag, the child may need a lesson in imagination. The boy who no longer plays with his dump truck may love your suggestion to build a garage out of a plastic laundry basket using a cookie sheet for a ramp.

- Help your children avoid toy confusion as well as become responsible by teaching them how to put toys away. Show the children how to store small pieces in clear plastic boxes or jars. Help them label containers, first with pictures then words.

- Share the joy! Christmas coming? Give your child the opportunity to delight in *giving*. Buy and wrap at least one toy for a child less fortunate than your own—and involve your child in the process while you explain the true meaning of Christmas. Involve older children in decisions about where the family charity dollars should go this year.

- Remember what every child needs and wants from adults: affection and attention. Neither costs money. You don't have to shop for them or gift wrap them!

In summary, Children need three "C's" from their parents and their world: **Connections**—closeness to parents and other loving family members; **Chores**—so they feel valued and important around the house; and **Community**—neighbors, friends, teachers to care for and receive caring attention from. They do not need a nearly infinite number of consumer goods to be happy. "Things" like toys will never be a substitute for connections, chores, and community.

What About Toy Guns?

First of all, **guns don't belong in homes!** Guns used to be expensive and were designed and used only for hunting or target shooting. Today guns are plentiful, cheap, and designed to kill people, lots of people. Sad fact # 1: Many homes with children have multiple automatic weapons. Sad fact # 2: Many homes with children lack adult supervision especially after school until the parents get home from work.

We live in a violent world. Unfortunately humankind has not evolved to the point where all disputes are peacefully negotiated; where we use our brains not our brawn (and those extensions of brawn, the weapons we have invented) to solve problems between people and nations; where empathy prevents our hurting anyone because we would not wish to be so hurt ourselves.

Parents cannot prevent their children from knowing about weapons, violence, and war. And, let's face it, there is plenty of violence in the books your children might read including the Bible and fairy tales. But parents can stick by their guns (pun intended) when it comes to war toys. Today's kids have enough to play with without guns and violent computer games.

Practical Suggestions:

- It is perfectly OK to tell your children you will not buy any toy guns or other war toys. Children can thrive in homes without war toys. My impression is that thoughtful parents today are making a conscious effort both to forbid toy guns and to preach against violence.

- You don't have to allow other children to bring guns into your house. Make a game as well as a values lesson out of this matter. Tell children who come to visit that they have to check guns at the door like the cowboys used to do in the Wild West. Point out that you don't like guns because they hurt people.

- Talk about violent toys to teach children. Ask questions—and encourage questions—like, "What does a gun do to people?"

- Use every opportunity you have to interpret the world for your children in terms of your own anti-violent feelings. When your child sees or mentions violence, use the opportunity to say, "How would you feel if that happened to you?" or "Can you think of a better way to solve that argument?"

- Provide your children with many play opportunities that are non-violent. Play can and should be constructive and creative. Buy building blocks and books, crayons and construction paper, hand puppets and puzzles.

- Limit TV and, whenever possible, watch TV with your children so you can change channels and/or interpret what they see in terms of the your family's values.

- Do not despair if your kids turn peaceful toys into war games or pretend toy trucks are tanks. Such play does not mean aggressive or anti-social behavior in later years.

- Do not worry about turning your child into a "sissy" if you forbid war toys. Personal courage in a child is much more closely related to strong feelings of autonomy and self-worth ("I can do it all by myself!") than the presence of toy guns.

Limit TV, Video Games, Computers

ParenTips:

- *Limit TV to One Hour per Day and Monitor What Your Child Is Watching.*

- *Limit Video Games and Computer Usage.*

- *Model TV-Free Behavior for Your Children.*

I'm definitely on the limit-TV-bandwagon. Yes, TV can be a valuable resource for children. It certainly can be educational and can widen children's horizons. It can expose children, especially those who do not live in a big city, to wonderful cultural events they might not otherwise see, like opera or the Olympics. It can be diversionary at times of forced inactivity like recovering from a broken leg.

But there are many more ways TV can be harmful to children. I have called TV an **"Environmental Pollutant."** I feel quite strongly that, as in the case of other pollutants, children are more susceptible than adults to the deleterious effects of TV.

The American Academy of Pediatrics has long held that TV be limited to one to two hours daily. Obviously not too many parents are listening because the average time spent watching TV is over 27 hours per week for two-to-five-year-olds and over 23 hours per week for six-to-eleven-year-olds. (Dietz, William and Strasburger, Victor. "Children, Adolescents, and Television." Current Problems in Pediatrics, January 1991.) The AAP now recommends no TV at all for children under two.

The numbers get more worrisome when they are totaled. Children spend more time in front of the TV set than in any other activity except sleeping. By age 18, children and adolescents will have spent more hours watching TV (15,000 to 18, 000) than in the classroom (12,000). By the time they are 70, today's children will have watched seven years of TV! (Strasburger, Victor. "Children, Adolescents, and Television." Pediatrics in Review, April, 1992.)

Well, you might say, TV is part of our culture. So what if children watch so much of it? My main objections and concerns:

- **Violence** abounds on TV. It was estimated that a child would have to see all of Shakespeare's 37 plays to see the same number of violent acts (54) there are in three nights of prime time! (Trelease, Jim. The Read-Aloud Handbook New York: Penguin Books, 1982) And the evidence that TV violence increases the likelihood of aggressive behavior in children, especially in boys, is compelling.

  We know that when children view violence they exhibit an increase in violent behavior and we know that TV fosters imitative behavior in children, which can be dangerous.

  Is TV society's mirror or model when it comes to violence? Probably both, but violence was formerly portrayed in the theater as tragedy or slapstick; on TV children see the blood spurting but rarely see anyone mourning the death. There is no way watching such deceptive realism is good for children.

- Undue exposure to what I call **unrealistic sex,** with 14,000 explicit references to sex per year and less than 175 references to contraception or sexually transmitted diseases. On the soaps, mention of sex between unmarried partners is 24 times more common than sex between married partners. (Strasburger)

- **Consumerism** has reached new lows: there are now more than 70 program-length commercials to sell toy products to children. (This type of marketing to innocent children has been referred to recently as "electronic child abuse.") Nearly all of the best-selling toys on today's market are based on TV programs or movies.

  Consumerism is more heavily promoted by TV than by any other medium. TV advertising specifically aimed at children tells them that children should have every toy they wish for and that their cupboards should be filled with every brand of sugared cereal and candy.

- **TV encourages poor health habits.** Big couch potatoes grow from little couch potatoes! Couch potatoes not only aren't exercising but they are being exposed to junk food commercials. We all know that overeating without exercise is the formula for obesity. Even more troublesome is that children with elevated cholesterol levels watched more hours of TV than control children with normal cholesterol levels.

  Prime time programs contain an average of 4.8 mentions of food per 30-minute segment. Sixty percent of the references are for low-nutrient beverages and sweets. Of course this nicely parallels the fact that 35 percent of the commercials are for food!

  In addition, people shown on TV— from news anchors to actors to those who spout commercials—are almost all thin, which could even be contributing to the increase in the incidence of anorexia nervosa.

- TV is to my way of thinking a *colossal waste of time.* Childhood should be a prime time for active learning, talking, reading, thinking, integrating, consolidating, dreaming, imagining, and interacting with others.

- There is an increasing body of evidence that being exposed to *large quantities of TV and video games affects the way children think and learn.* Children who habitually take in information from pictures and "sound bites" don't seem to be able to pay sustained attention to teachers, follow directions, problem-solve, or read with understanding. Further, children seem to need "special effects" in the classroom in order to interest them in a topic. A long book is too much for them to tackle.

  We are raising a generation of "a-literates"—people who know how to read but choose not to. They want to get all information the instant, pre-digested way. As a matter of fact, recent studies show that TV watching more than one or two hours a day has a deleterious effect on reading scores.

- **Stereotyping** abounds. Entire groups of people like the elderly are shown as feeble or are under-represented. The cartoons stereotype villains as foreigners. Teen-age girls are shown obsessed with makeup, shopping, and boys while intelligent girls are portrayed as misfits. Women are portrayed in both programs and commercials as traditional homemakers, though more than 60 percent of mothers are employed outside the home.

- What bothers me most about TV is its utter *passivity*. One day when my grandchildren were visiting, all the grown-ups were enjoying another cup of coffee. I happened to notice the faces of my two grandsons, who were sitting on the floor with their eyes glued to the cartoons on the TV screen. Their eyes did not move; they were practically in a trance, zombie-like. I had a flashback to my young daughter reading a book and I remembered how her eyes darted back and forth across the page. She was *actively reading*. My grandsons were passively watching. A big difference!

What do I suggest parents do? I don't recommend throwing out the TV set because there are some programs that every child should watch, like men walking on the moon or the opening ceremonies of the Olympics. But no parent would knowingly expose their child to a pollutant in the environment that could be harmful. **Parents can and should control TV in their household.**

- Remember, TV is an appliance which comes with an on/off switch like a food processor. Don't be afraid to **turn off the TV!** One family I know actually unplugs the set and places it in the closet after the children have watched their allotted TV. Do not leave the TV set on all the time so that it becomes a continuous background murmur and glow to everything going on in your house.

- **Limit the amount of TV** your child can watch. I recommend one hour maximum per school day and two on weekend days.

- Carefully **monitor** the content of the programs you permit your child to watch. Sex and violence are not child's play.

- Whenever possible **watch TV with your children.** It's important that you be around to interpret what the child sees in terms of your family values. This is necessary even if you forbid adult type programs, because the six o'clock news can contain references to violence, sex, lawlessness, etc. If you are there you can explain what you find objectionable. "Our family would never do that!"

- Do not let young children watch MTV! Music videos combine all the dreadful things about TV: sex, violence (especially violence against women), alienation from society, and stereotyping.

- **Encourage your children to lead active lives** off the couch. Let them invite friends over to play; expose them to sports; give them music lessons; teach them how to play board and card games; expect them to do chores; encourage them to do art work by having supplies available at home.

- Be a **good role model.** Don't watch a lot of TV yourself. Let your children see you reading, engaged in sports, etc. Children are more apt to do what we do than what we say.

- **Don't** be suckered into buying your children the program-advertised TV toys—or at least limit the number you buy.

- If you can't watch TV with your children, **screen** the programs or **rent** suitable videos. Always know what your child is watching. Do not let your children play "channel roulette" or they may end up watching terrible things.

- If you are busy and tired working parents who need some feet-up time in front of the TV set but can't find any suitable programming, rent an old movie and watch it on the VCR. There are some wonderful old comedies and musicals available and some of the old dramas and westerns are suitable for children. To find out which films will be suitable for children and will also interest them, use a movie/video guide (there are several in paperback) or patronize only a video store that labels films as suitable for kids.

- If you are a tired mother who uses TV as an electronic babysitter while you fix dinner (I was on of those tired mothers myself), there are better solutions. Although a couple of hours of TV a day will not do irrevocable harm to the children of a tired mother, you can teach the children how to cook so they can help you in the kitchen. Even a four-year-old can set a table. Alternatively, let the children read to you while you are cooking.

Video Games and Excessive Time at the Computer

OK, video games are a part of our culture and help children with hand-eye coordination. But, for many of the same reasons I advocate limiting TV, I strongly advise parental limits to video games.

Violence, sex stereotyping, and overall stupidity are awful but are the least of my worries. The **displacement** effect can be enormous. Children addicted to video games are not reading, not doing homework, not exercising, not interacting with other children.

Limit the games to an hour a day. Encourage your children to read and play outdoors. They'll be happier and healthier!

Do I dare write anything against the computer while typing on one? What if it loses my document! But seriously, children and computers do not make a good marriage. Yes, computer skills are important, but reading skills are more important. Don't let your child overdo computer time in lieu of reading time. You parents who work at home on your computers: let your kids see you read a book once in a while!

I've already talked about violence of computer games and the negative displacement effect of young human mammals spending more time in front of a screen than with people. My final computer concern is unsupervised access to the Internet. **Know what your child is doing and seeing on-line!** There are simply awful things out there that no child should see or read. Monitor that monitor! When your children protest in the name of privacy, tell them you **care!** Dialogue and loving attention to what your child is doing can give your child the strength to say no to pornography or violence at a friend's house.

Painful Realities/Difficult Situations

ParenTips:

- *Be Honest.*

- *Model How to Deal with Painful Feelings.*

- *Encourage a Child to Talk about Painful Feelings.*

- *Empower Children by Giving Them a Chance to Help and Be Involved.*

All children will one day be confronted with **painful realities** like **death, dangers, disasters,** and **divorce.** They may also be exposed to **difficult situations** like chronic illness or disability, a grandfather with Alzheimer's, Daddy losing his job, a relative going to jail, etc.

Regardless of which painful reality confronts your child, your approach should be the same. Parents should always **be honest, model how to deal with feelings, give the child a chance to talk about the situation,** and **empower your child in every way you can.**

Death

We all want to protect our children from the pain of dealing with death—either the death of a loved one or thoughts about their own death—but we can't. Death is an inescapable part of life.

It's a good idea to start "death education" early, just as we start teaching about sex early. And, as is true for sexuality education, the most important thing we can do is to show our children that each of us is an "askable parent."

Whenever a child begins to ask questions about death—usually prompted by exposure to a death in an animal or person—expect questions like, "Will I die too?" or "How do we get it alive again?" or "What happens to Puppy after we bury him?" Parents should answer such questions honestly, imparting a bit more information than the child is ready for. Information beyond the child's understanding may not get processed but the child realizes that death is a subject that can be talked about.

Bring up the subject on your own. When the family watches the news on TV or a movie in which someone dies, start a discussion. The library has many books for young children dealing with death, usually of a relative.

A child's understanding of death is developmentally determined. Before the age of six or so children usually think of death as reversible. For example, they may think grown-ups can still communicate with the deceased. But young children certainly experience grief. They may also feel guilt about having possibly been responsible for the death of a close relative, because they will invariably remember feeling angry at the person and worry that their negative thoughts magically "killed" the person.

All children at one time or another will express a variation on one of these worries: "Am I going to die?" "What will happen to me if Mommy or Daddy dies?" Parents have to deal with both issues honestly but humanely: "Everybody dies but you won't die for a very long time. There will always be someone to take care of you."

The next question will be, "Do I really have to die when I am old?" Once again, honesty: "Every living thing eventually dies but you won't die for a very long time." It can take a child quite a while to process difficult or new information, so expect to repeat such reassuring statements as needed.

Avoid euphemisms. Don't say that the dead person is asleep, or that God took Grandpa, or that Grandma went on a very long trip and is never coming back. It's easy to see how a child given such explanations could become afraid of sleep, God, and travel.

Obviously what you tell your child will be rooted in your own belief system. Though you believe that Grandpa's soul is in Heaven and tell this to the child, it's important to add that his body is in a coffin in the ground.

Funerals

There is no age at which taking a child to a funeral is right or wrong. Children over seven who can understand the permanence of death should be involved in the family grieving process. A funeral makes the death seem real and gives the child a chance to both honor the dead person and feel a sense of community because others are sharing the grief.

A younger child will not experience the important sense of closure that the funeral can impart. However, if the young child is not likely to be disruptive and the child's parents will not themselves be so overcome by grief as to disturb the child, by all means take the child to the funeral.

Prepare children ahead of time as to what will happen at the funeral, including lowering the coffin and covering it with earth. Someone familiar to the child but not involved in the ceremony should be with the child at all times to help the child with the grief, to answer any questions ("No, Grandpa doesn't feel anything any more.") or to remove the child if the child gets too upset.

Even if the child doesn't remember attending the funeral, talking about the child's presence there ("Remember the rainbow we saw the day we said good-bye to Grandma at her funeral?") can help the child remember the dead person and deal with any lingering concerns.

Grieving

Children grieve differently than adults. Some may seem quite callous when told of a death and neither cry nor seem concerned. But children who lose a loved one have the same strong emotions to deal with: guilt and anger. The child may exhibit a drop in school performance, behavior problems, lack of appetite, sleeplessness. Because these symptoms could occur weeks or even months after the death, parents should realize the possible association with the death and seek counseling help if indicated.

Parents can help by sharing their *own* grief with the child. A brave front is never as helpful as the quiet sharing of tears and memories. Let the child know that it's OK to grieve and cry and feel bad. Help the child come to understand that feelings of grief diminish and that you both will come out of this sad space.

Honor the love your child had for the dead person by helping keep memories alive with photographs, videos, or audio tapes. Observe the anniversary of the death by quiet personal remembrances or meaningful gestures like planting a tree to honor the memory.

Impending Death

When should you tell a child that a loved one is dying? I believe in telling the child the truth and, depending upon the child's age and the circumstances, giving the child a chance to say good-bye.

You don't have to hit the child over the head with the bad news. Start by telling the child Grandpa is very sick. If the child asks, "Is he going to die?" be honest. If the child does not ask, you can give him or her a chance to get used to Grandpa's illness before mentioning death. Always prepare the child for what to expect when he or she visits, especially if the person's appearance is changing or medical paraphernalia is in use.

Do not try to conceal your own grief when you tell the child. Better you cry together and talk about how sad it is that Grandpa is dying than give the impression that grown-ups hide their feelings. Hidden feelings, not honest answers, are what can harm a child who thinks: "What is wrong? Why is everybody so upset? Did I do something wrong?"

Sharing grief with your child does three important things: it gives the child permission to grieve, it gives the message that you consider the child mature enough to deal with such issues, and it gives the child a sense of closeness and community with the most important persons in the child's life, the parents.

Death of a Child

This is the toughest task. You may expect to be asked something like, "Why is Jimmy dying? He's not old." Your child really needs information. However painful it is, tell your child that sometimes children get so sick that they cannot be made better again and they die. Go on to explain, "Dying at this age is very rare, what Jimmy has isn't catching, you are not sick and you are not dying."

Be sure to add how terrible this makes you feel. Cry, if you can, and hug your child. Give the child plenty of time to express his or her own sadness. Explain to your child how people talk to someone whose loved one is dying. Ask your child if he or she can think of anything the sick child might like to have.

Use your family's religious beliefs about heaven or an afterlife to help your child deal with the death of a friend. But, trust me, what will help your child most is talking about the death.

Encourage children who are old enough to visit the sick friend and attend the funeral. Help the child memorialize the friend. Plant a tree, make a contribution in the child's memory, have the children draw a picture of their friend, or make a card for his parents.

Your child can learn a valuable lesson from you by hearing what you say to the sick child's mother. "My heart goes out to you and I don't have the words to express how badly I feel." To reach out you have to do only four things: look the person in the eye, touch the person, tell the person how sorry you are, and ask how you can help.

Dangers

Parents today must make their children appropriately **aware of realistic dangers** at the same time that they must instill in their children a **sense of personal confidence** and the **skills** to interact with other human beings.

How wonderful it would be if parents could honestly feel and say to their children that the world is a safe—not scary—place!

It's easy to reassure preschoolers that there are no monsters under the bed. But it is difficult to tell children that there are bad people out there who can hurt them.

How can parents deal with potential dangers to their children in today's world? How can parents protect their children from danger, and yet allow them appropriate freedom of action and freedom from fear?

- Parents can learn to **assess dangers realistically** utilizing probability. If your child does not use a seat belt or bike helmet or if there is no smoke alarm in the house, your child is in danger of injury or death. Kidnapping or molestation by a stranger is a very remote occurrence.

- Work together with other parents to **make the neighborhood safe** for children. We value privacy so much that we overlook the importance of what a neighborhood should be. All of us should look out for the safety and welfare of all the kids. Is Johnny riding his bike recklessly? Tell his parents. Are there suspicious strangers hanging around? Call the police.

- **Model appropriately safe behaviors** for your children. Wear your seat belt, lock the car doors, park in well-lighted areas. Make these actions very matter-of-fact, like brushing your teeth. This helps your child realize that living safely is sensible, not something we do out of fear.

- Even though you must tell your children that there are bad people in the world, be sure to point out that **most people are good.** Be specific. Most people do not hurt children, they help them—people like teachers, policemen, neighbors, doctors (shots excepted!), bus drivers, etc.

- When something bad happens—like the kidnapping of Polly Klaas—**talk about it.** If your child hears about something bad on TV, interpret the significance for the child. Don't lecture or pontificate. Instead, encourage the child to talk and ask questions because your child may not have a realistic understanding of the situation. Ask pertinent questions like, "Can you think of things our city could do to prevent gang violence?" Brainstorm together ways to keep family members safe.

- **Role-play** with your child what to do in potentially dangerous situations. What if somebody in a car asks directions? (Stay a safe distance away from the car.) What if a stranger asks you to help look for his lost puppy? (Refuse and quickly walk away.)

- Have a **family "password."** If **anyone** tells your child, "Your Mom sent me because she can't pick you up at school today," the child must ask for the family secret word before getting in the car. Use the password system even if you ask a well-known neighbor to pick up the child because this is a way of teaching your child the importance of the password.

- Teach your child that a stranger is a person you don't know well even if you have seen the person around. Explain who trusted adults are because you won't always be around. Ask the child to make a list of adults he or she can and should trust.

- **Teach** your child this safety rule that is easy to understand and obey: **Never go ANYWHERE with ANYBODY unless you ask the grown-up in charge first.** "Don't go with a stranger!" doesn't work. Maybe they did just that at the dentist last week, and were praised for acting grown-up when they went into the office with the hygienist. And besides the stranger rule gives the child license to go with everybody whom the child does recognize.

- Be sure your child knows the family's full names, address, phone number and how and when to use 911.

- Whenever you go to a crowded place like the mall have a designated meeting place in case you become separated.

- Teach your child how to get help if scared or lost. Role-play what your child would say to a policeman or bus driver.

- Teach children to travel in pairs, walk in well-lighted areas, avoid deserted areas, and act "powerful" rather than afraid or worried ("I whistle a happy tune!") when approached by strangers.

- Don't overdo the fear trip. There is a serious downside to overprotective parenting because the child can grow up feeling: **1)** the world is a scary place, and **2)** I can't trust myself to meet the world's challenges on my own.

Sexual Dangers

Parents must help children deal with realistic dangers of sexual predators like pedophiles without making the children fearful of adults.

Explaining what life is really like is one of our tasks as parents. Do this in the same way you explain what lightning and thunder are. It's scary but here's how we deal with it.

Don't raise fearful children. Instead raise **wary** children who understand there is evil as well as good in the world, and are **empowered** to protect themselves.

The sad but true fact is that persons who molest or sexually abuse children are **almost always known to the child.** In as many as 40 percent of the cases the perpetrator is **related** to the child: father, stepfather, sibling, cousin.

Contrary to the fears of many parents, a random attack on a child by a perverted stranger who just moved into the neighborhood is very rare. The truth is, trusted caretakers of children such as their coaches and teachers and leaders of childhood activities are more likely to be the perpetrators of sexual abuse.

In a sense children make perfect victims of sexual abuse because of the way we socialize them. We tell children to respect their elders, to obey grown-ups like parents and teachers, and to do what they are told. By nature children are trusting, curious, and want attention and affection. No wonder they can be easy prey to a grown-up who has a position of authority and takes the time to build up trust by pretending to be really interested in the child or what the child likes to do.

Suggestions for helping your child deal with the fact that there may be grown-ups out there that want to do bad things to them:

- Teach your child, from the very first bath, that he or she is **special.** Keep telling the child it's important to take care of that special self and special body.

- Teach your children, starting from early toddlerhood, that their body is **private** and **belongs to nobody else.** Give the child the right words, first by naming body parts correctly and second, by teaching the child that private means the parts covered by the bathing suit. Respect the child's desire for privacy in the bathroom.

- Don't you or anyone else in the family demand a kiss or a hug. Ask.

- Teach your child about **good touch/bad touch.** A good touch **feels** good like a hug you want. A bad touch is a hit or a kick that hurts or a touch on a part of your body that's private. Sometimes you don't know how you feel about a touch so we call that a **confusing touch.** Tell the child, "If you have a bad or confusing touch say 'No!' **Only you know how you feel about the way your body is touched.**

- Teach your child to say "No!" as loudly as possible to any bad touch..

- Teach your child the difference between a **bad secret** that makes you feel uncomfortable and a **good secret** like a surprise party. Parents should be told bad secrets. Don't criticize a child for tattling.

- Help your children understand that **telling** is OK. They will be better able to do this if they **trust** you. Tell them you won't ever blame them and will always help them be safe. If your child ever tells you about an abusive incident, be sure the first thing you say is, **"It's not your fault!"**

- Never punish children for telling you what's on their minds. Don't belittle their fears or disregard their ideas. Freedom of expression—although not freedom of action—is a gift every parent should bestow.

- Be cautious about any adults, no matter how trustworthy you consider them to be by reason of their status or profession, who take a special or prolonged interest in your child. Spend some time observing your child with this adult and use your gut feeling. If you have any question about the adult's motives, take your child out of the situation.

- Always **listen** to a child who is reluctant to do something or go somewhere. Sort it out. Is the kid worried about homesickness or is there a problem with the camp-out leader?

- Do not fall into the trap of thinking the child is making up stories about abuse or molestation. This rarely happens.

Disasters—Natural or Man-Made

What about dealing with a highly publicized disaster, especially one involving children like the bombing of the federal building in Oklahoma City or an earthquake?

- **Be honest.** Do not try to conceal the truth, lie, gloss over the facts, or pretend nothing happened.

- **Express your own feelings.** "What a terrible thing to bomb innocent children!" In order for children to learn how to deal with strong feelings they need to watch how grown-ups do it. Do not give a child the message that emotions are best concealed or ignored.

- **Always explain that you will keep your child safe.** It's important to say that what happened was far away, that it was done by terrible people who will be caught and punished, and that most people in the world are good.

    The bright child may ponder, "But, Dad, the parents in Oklahoma wanted to keep their kids safe but they died anyway." You should tell your child that's why everybody feels so bad, because innocent children whose parents loved them were hurt. But everybody, including the President, is going to work very hard to make sure that such things don't happen in the future. The terrorists will be found and punished. Then repeat that you will do everything in your power to keep your child safe always.

- **Encourage your child to talk about what happened.** Ask questions that require a thinking answer like, "How do you suppose that Mommy feels?" "What do you suppose the rescuers think when they go into that building?"

    Encourage young children to draw pictures or act out the rescue or hospital scene with dolls. Older children? Suggest they write a poem or story about what happened.

- **Empower your child.** Suggest things the child can do to help like send cards, collect money from all the cousins to give to victims, write letters to the rescue teams thanking them, write to the President asking him to fight against terrorism. Older children might do a project about terrorism. Empowerment comes from getting involved and doing something.

- Be sure to **give plenty of hugs and cuddles.** When we are grieving we need human contact. Hugs are a palpable demonstration of your love and your children need to know they are loved.

- **Turn off the TV.** Don't bombard your child—or yourself—with repeated horrors.

Divorce

Divorce causes everybody involved to feel awful because it can mean a breaking-up of just about everything: marriage, family, household, friendships. In addition to these big losses, there is often a profound sense of failure. And if that were not enough, there is often agonizing guilt about what the divorce will do to the children.

Divorce is stressful for everybody—mother, father and children. Successful outcome for children after a divorce is more likely when children have a stable, close relationship with *both* parents, who are no longer feuding.

I rarely talk about parental sacrifice for children because I don't believe in parental martyrdom. As a matter of fact, martyrs make lousy parents. But in the case of divorce, because the disruption is so difficult for a young child, I ask parents to search their hearts for those sacrifices they can make for the sake of the child.

Here are the Heins' Six Commandments for divorced parents:

- **Never bad-mouth the other parent**

- Tell the child repeatedly that: **1) The divorce is NOT your fault; 2)** It's OK to love **both** parents; **3) It's OK to feel sad and angry** because the family is breaking up; **4) There's nothing to be ashamed about,** the divorce is between the parents; **5)** You will ***always be taken care of.***

- Keep lines of **communication** with the ex-spouse wide open so you can always do what is in the best interest of the child.

- Keep routines and rules reasonably **consistent** no matter which parent the child is with. Tell children what's going to happen and keep their lives as predictable as possible.

- ***Never put your child in the middle.*** Assure your children they will never have to take sides—and mean what you say. Never use your child to take messages of your anger or grief to the other parent.

- Run, don't walk, to get **counseling** help so you will "be there" for your child.

Difficult Situations

"Not in front of the children!" is an expression we've all heard and most of us have used. But you cannot protect your children from life's difficulties. You **can** provide your children with the strengths they will need to deal with these difficulties.

Whether the difficulty is grandfather with Alzheimer's Disease, Daddy being "downsized," disability, or chronic illness in a loved one, the parent's tasks are the same. Let's use grandpa's Alzheimer's as the model.

Don't try to conceal a family tragedy from a child. It doesn't work. The child will know something is wrong and often will imagine something is worse than it is.

I remember my own daughter saying to me, "Mommy, what's the matter?" trying to smooth the frown off my forehead with her little fingers. I thought I was successfully concealing a king-size sadness I did not share with her.

When I told my daughter that Great-Grandpa was sick, she answered, "I thought you were mad at me!" I learned two valuable lessons from that incident: children are exquisitely sensitive to their parents' moods and children are very prone to thinking that they caused the negative mood.

Let the children see your sadness and explain why you feel that way. "Grandpa is very sick. His brain doesn't work normally any more and he can't take care of himself. This makes me feel very sad because I love Grandpa."

Keep in mind the developmental age of the child when you explain what is happening. Try to use words the child will understand. Explain terms and interpret. "Grandpa will go to the home so he can be cared for. He needs to be cared for day and night and Grandma can't manage. We will put pictures of all of us where Grandpa can see them and we'll go visit so Grandpa won't be lonely."

Don't feel you have to go into minute detail unless the child asks for more information. The rule is to be honest but brief. Often the child is helped more by hearing an explanation of the "category" than the specifics. Some children just want to know that Grandpa is sick and will have to go to a nursing home. Others want to know if it hurts or what happens to the brain to cause this. The less you say, especially when you first talk about the problem, the easier it is for the child to formulate his or her questions, which help you learn what the child is thinking.

Encourage the child to talk about the issue and ask questions. If the child doesn't ask, be sure to explain three things: **1)** What is happening to Grandpa won't happen to the child. **2)** The child didn't cause it in any way. (Young children may think their misbehavior or even a negative thought magically caused the tragedy). **3)** There's nothing to be ashamed of. Lots of people have disabled grandfathers and he couldn't help what happened.

Encourage mastery of the situation. Give the child words to explain what is happening to Grandpa to friends. Help children find books about aging or how the brain works. Suggest an older child write a report on Alzheimer's disease for school. Play dolls with a younger child and pretend to make Grandpa comfortable by feeding or hugging the doll.

Talk together as a family about who Grandpa used to be. Encourage your spouse to talk about what Grandpa was like years ago. Put up pictures of Grandpa before he was sick and try to keep the good memories alive.

As far as visits to the nursing home are concerned, yes take your children to visit because it is better for them to see reality than to imagine it. But don't force them to go. If a child doesn't want to visit, ask the child to make a drawing you will take to Grandpa so the child can feel loving and caring even though not yet brave.

Manners

ParenTips:

- *Model, Instruct, Suggest Mannerly Behaviors from Toddlerhood.*

- *Many Reminders Will Be Needed.*

- *Show and Tell the Necessary Conventions like Meeting People, Table and Restaurant Manners, Telephone Behavior, and Thank-you Notes.*

Humans are complex social animals. We cannot get along by ourselves; we need other members of our species around. The polite conventions and graces we use keep us from hurting each other so we can remain together. Human interaction is too important to leave to chance and possible breakdown—manners are not called "social conventions" for nothing.

Although the world is a more casual place than it once was, people must still interact with each other and always will. People will always need to interact kindly so that they will be treated kindly in return.

Part of your job description as a parent is to teach manners to your child.

An infant is not born with manners and must be taught how to behave with politeness and courtesy. But the child is born with a built-in desire to please the parents and the wise parent uses this to gently guide the child toward the paths of courtesy.

The dictionary defines manners as polite conventions or polite ways of social behavior. I like to think of manners as the quintessence of human communication because manners are based on **love, concern,** and **empathy**—all very human characteristics.

Human communication starts at birth with the first eye contact. The stage for this communication is set before the baby is born because the newborn baby is preprogrammed to prefer to look at human faces. Self-love is the next step; the child needs to become aware of his or her self and must appreciate that self in order to develop empathy.

Manners must be based on this awareness of, and love of, self. Then the child can become aware of the selves of others and come to realize that these other selves can be hurt just as the child's own self can.

Caring is manners and manners are caring.

How Children Learn Manners

How can parents best teach a child the polite conventions we call manners? When should a parent start? Children learn best through imitation. If they are surrounded by people who love each other, do not wish to hurt each other, and follow the "rules" for courtesy, the child will **model this mannerful behavior.**

But children learn in other ways too. They learn by **instruction** and **suggestions,** and **reminders.** Some parents today seem almost afraid to make a direct suggestion when it comes to a matter of discipline or manners. Not to worry. The gentle suggestion and the quiet reminder are both effective ways to reinforce what the child is learning through imitation.

There is absolutely nothing wrong with reminding a toddler to say "Please" and "Thanks." We hear a lot about four-letter words today, but these six-letter ones are much more useful. A monosyllabic exclamation may get someone's attention but will not otherwise do much for human communication!

Children learn at a rapid rate, but until they cognitively understand the reasons for courtesy, they will need to be reminded to say "Please." Many times.

What about the advanced course in manners? How important is it to teach children adult manners and when should parents start? I feel strongly that parents have the task of preparing their children to be able to live anyplace in our complex world. Basic good manners are not elitist; they are necessary everywhere.

When you have finished your job of parenting, your child should be able to walk through any door on earth and feel both comfortable and self-confident.

The child who has not learned the social conventions will not feel comfortable inside this hypothetical door.

Some of the important conventions include introductions, the firm handshake, table and restaurant manners, telephone manners, and thank-you notes. Obviously you won't begin to teach these graces until the child is developmentally ready.

Interacting with Others

A preschooler is often shy or apprehensive when meeting new people so let the child just observe the new person until the child is ready to "warm up." A young child should never be forced to interact, shake hands, hug, or speak until he or she is ready to do so. The shy child will take longer to get used to a new person.

Ideally, all lessons in the social graces are preceded by an empathy lesson. "How would you feel?" is a good way to help the child understand what courtesy is all about.

But empathy is more than understanding. It is the ability to pick up cues from people about whether they are comfortable or not. Praise your children when they demonstrate this sensitivity. Especially boys, who seem less adept than girls at picking up these cues.

We now know that even children as young as one year of age can demonstrate generous, caring behavior when they notice that someone is sad or tired or hurt. Yes, kids can be totally narcissistic and selfish sometimes, but they also have a caring side.

Parents can and should help nurture this nurturing side of their children. Tell them how much you care about their caring behavior. "How nice of you to give a toy to Jenny when she was crying. I'm so happy that you think about other people's feelings!"

Also make it quite clear you *do not care for* any mean or unkind behavior. "Calling Josh a baby hurt his feelings! What you said was mean!"

In addition to praising caring behavior it's a good idea to praise special kindnesses a child shows. "You gave your allowance to buy food for the homeless. That makes me very proud!" And finally give your child opportunities to practice caring by involving them in appropriate volunteer and charitable activities.

When the child is old enough, specific instructions about meeting new people are in order. I think it's a good idea to teach children of both genders to shake hands when they are introduced to new people. When? It depends. By five or six children are aware that certain grown-up behaviors are or will be expected of them.

Model the appropriate behavior first: look the new person right in the eyes and hold out your right hand. Then tell your child he or she is grown-up enough to start doing this grown-up behavior. Next role-play together, pretending to meet lots of new people. Be creative: pretend to be the President, Mickey Mouse, or the latest TV craze. When the next appropriate occasion occurs, gently remind your child to **look** and **hold out the right hand.**

Niceties like saying "I'm glad to meet you" and remembering who gets introduced to whom can come later when these basics are firmly in place.

Don't push the shy child, who may find just **looking** at a new person agonizing. Instead continue to role-play and tell the child that when he or she is ready you'll start with real instead of pretend introductions. However, many children who act shy are shying away from new people because they have not yet learned what they are supposed to do.

A child who is in middle school should have mastered the **firm** handshake, the direct **look** and the smile and appropriate words that go with an introduction.

Table Manners

Children are certainly not born with table manners, but they are born with a desire to please their parents. A gentle reminder to use a fork instead of the fingers or to wipe the mouth usually works—for the moment. It's understandable why parents get discouraged when they repeat the same gentle reminder for the umpteenth time. But it takes a long time for a young child to learn all the rules, to remember when to use them, and to understand why they are important.

Table manners are not trivial. Eating together, at least for some meals, is an important part of most family's togetherness. Eating with care, delicacy, and restraint is one of the attributes that makes us human and different from animals. Watching someone with gross eating habits is repulsive to most of us.

Food itself has special significance. People have deep feelings about food and all major religions have something to say about food and meals. Most of us feel that wasting food is wrong. Watching little children play with food or throw it around can be more disturbing to some of us than we realize—until we see our toddler do it. And nobody wants to pick up from the floor food that a child has deliberately thrown down, or spend time cooking only to see the food thrown out.

As parents we **1)** don't want our children to eat repulsively at our table and **2)** don't want them to grow up and be socially ostracized because of the way they eat. But we also don't want to turn mealtimes into a nag-fest. What's a parent to do?

A baby does not perceive the difference between food and other play materials. In the second half of the first year babies begin to self-feed using the only utensil they can manage, the fingers.

Messy as it is, food play at this age is important and should be overlooked if not encouraged. Squishing the fingers through mashed potatoes before licking the fingers is, for the baby, an aesthetic, exploratory, and learning experience—as well as a nutritional one! The parents' role is to try to enjoy this developmental stage and clean up cheerfully. (I put newspapers under the high chair. One mother put a cap on her son's head, which was easier than shampooing three times a day!)

Another developmental issue has to do with the length of time a young child can be expected to sit still. I don't believe in making children under four or five sit at the table when they are through eating, especially if the parents like to linger. Let the children play quietly in the kitchen or dining room until you are finished.

By the time the child is three, parents can expect reasonable table manners. Most children by now will use a spoon and fork pretty well although they may prefer finger foods so they don't have to worry about food spilling off the utensils.

A fun way to teach table manners to preschoolers is making a family game out of an occasional family meal. Use a tablecloth or pretty place mats, light candles if you like, have special foods, and generally make a big deal out of this "party." Use and demonstrate party manners like delicately wiping off a milk mustache with a corner of the napkin. Ask for and pass food with exquisite grace. Most kids get in the spirit of things and imitate these manners.

If you must correct your child at the table remember that there are two reasons we sit down at the table together: we eat the food we need to keep our bodies in good working order and we use the meal as a social occasion when we can talk together. Your goal is to keep the mealtime atmosphere pleasant so that the family can enjoy both aspects of eating. If you must point out that people keep their mouths closed while chewing, do it quietly and don't make a big fuss.

Restaurant Manners

Pick an appropriate restaurant where the service is prompt rather than leisurely and where something the child will enjoy is on the menu. Always bring along paper and crayons so the young child doesn't get restless before the food is served. If your child is cranky or hungry ask for some crackers.

Be involved with your child and notice whether the child is squirming or unhappy. Be prepared to use all your clever distraction tricks if they are needed. I played a drawing game with my children in which each of us in turn would draw part of a picture, some of which turned out pretty wild.

Do not permit the child to make undue noise, get out of the chair, or run around the restaurant because it is not safe and it is unfair to other customers. If the child won't stay seated, leave.

Minimum manners include sitting quietly, not screaming, not spitting, not throwing or playing with food. A child of three should be able to comply with these rules or be taken out of the restaurant, after one warning (because we all make mistakes). Even in a fast food restaurant, there are rules which parents must enforce: stay at your table and dump all food containers into the trash can.

As children get used to the requirements of restaurants you can take them to increasingly "fancy" places. Be sure they understand this is a special treat and privilege. Play games ahead of time about being seated, menu reading (both sides of the page), quiet conversation so other diners are not disturbed, etc.

As the children grow older they will be also invited to other people's homes to eat. School-age children are anxious to do the right thing so they will need some advanced lessons in table manners. Explain and demonstrate that when confronted with a lot of silverware at your plate you work from the outside in. The best advice you can give the child is to watch what the hostess is doing. If she picks up the chicken, that's OK. If she cuts it, follow suit.

Parties, family "special" meals and trips to restaurants are privileges, not rights. By the time your child is four, his or her manners should be acceptable in all these settings. If a four-year-old displays terrible manners, tell the child that those manners need work and you will not take the child to a restaurant again until the manners improve. And don't.

Telephone Manners

Telephone rules are important for two reasons: manners and safety. Toddlers love to answer the telephone. Because it's easy to lift up the receiver and say, "Hello!" and because it's magical to hear an answer, this is one of their first opportunities to master a grown-up task.

From the beginning start teaching that we talk slowly, clearly, and politely into the phone. Instruct your child to hand you the phone, to not interrupt or make noise when you are talking on the phone (this will take many months of instruction), and to not bang down the receiver.

As the child gets older teach our polite conventions ("Who is calling, please?") and teach the important safety rules about answering calls when the parents are away. Children should be taught to ALWAYS say, "My father can't come to the phone right now, may I take a message?"

As soon as he or she can write, a child should be taught to **write down all messages.** A second grader can write the person's name. By fourth or fifth grade children should be able to write the time of the call and the reason as well as the name.

Writing Manners

It's not so difficult to teach a child how to write a letter and a thank-you note. Start with preschoolers. Let them draw a picture and print their names on **your** letter to Grandma. As they get older buy them their own stationery and teach them how we write a letter with a salutation and signature.

Every gift deserves a thank-you note. A child who has learned to print his or her name should sign the note you write to Aunt Mary thanking her for the sweater she knitted for the child.

By the end of primary school children should write their own letters of thanks—and promptly. By graduation from middle school or Bar Mitzvah age children should be able to make their own lists, write and address each note, stamp and mail it, and check the gift giver's name off the list. The rule is: write the note before you use the gifts. Or no later than a month after receipt.

Chores

ParenTips:

- *Start Early.*

- *Gradually Increase Chores.*

- *Expect Children to Be Responsible for Chores.*

- *Do Not Pay for That Which Every Person Should Do in Exchange for the Privilege of Living in the Home.*

Everyone, regardless of gender, who lives in a house should be expected to do the following:

- Pick up after himself or herself.

- Keep his or her own space clean.

- Clean up after using common areas like bathtubs.

- Share in the daily, weekly, and seasonal household and yard chores.

- Learn to do simple cooking and survival food shopping.

Sons must be taught how to pick up after themselves and do such chores as laundry, vacuuming, cooking—and be expected to do them. Daughters must be taught how to do yard and garage chores and simple household repairs—and be expected to do them.

Our sons will live in a world where most women work outside the home. It is highly unlikely your sons will find—or be able to keep—mates if they don't know how to do household chores. Our daughters will live in a world where every woman must be able to care for herself, which means being able to survive without a man around the house. Stereotypes won't work in our brave new world.

All children must be taught how to be responsible. This means doing a chore without being told, being the kind of person on whom others in the family can count to take out the trash, feed the dog, or start dinner.

How do parents create a responsible house *mensch*—a useful Yiddish word which means "decent, responsible, caring person"—and prevent the genesis of a house slob?

- ● **Start early!**

- ● Although obviously what the child can or should do depends on the child's developmental level, starting in toddlerhood. Start with "Let's put our toys away!" and progress to, "Jody, you can't go out to play until you clean up the blocks!"

- ● The three-year-old child is incredibly anxious to please you and to imitate what you are doing. Take advantage of this! Three-year-olds can be taught to put dirty clothes in a hamper; hang up jackets, pajamas, and towels on reachable hooks; pick up and sort toys; straighten out magazines on a table; put silverware and pots away—and even empty the dishwasher if you use unbreakable dishes and store them on low shelves.

- ● Be patient and consistent because learning household tasks and learning how to assume responsibility for household tasks takes time and maturity.

- ● As the child grows increase the tasks and begin to give the child responsibility for doing them. This means the child does the task without being reminded to do so. It may take years (or even decades!) before everybody does chores without being reminded, but keep at it!

- ● When the children reach school age, start family meetings to find an equitable way to distribute and monitor the chores. Continue to be firm in your expectations that *everybody who lives in the house helps keep it clean.*

- ● Make a list of all household chores. Let the children choose which chores they wish to do—and draw lots for the rest. Set up an appointment with each child to show him or her how to do the chores. Ask the children to set up and keep a chart of who does what and when. Make a deadline column so it's clear to everybody that clearing the table means no later than fifteen minutes after dinner. Ask your children to devise a method of policing themselves and handling delinquency. Some families appoint a monitor for the week who makes sure all tasks are done and done on time.

- Explain carefully that failure to be responsible for the assigned chores has its logical consequences. If you didn't finish the dishes you can't go to the mall with Dad.

- Be sure to praise the children when chores are done responsibly. Be specific. "Putting away the groceries so quickly was a big help!" Leave notes not only to require action ("You didn't take out the trash so you are expected to clean the garage on Saturday") but also to praise a job done well and on time.

- Expect your children to do the tasks they have been assigned and to assume responsibility for these tasks. When you expect mature behavior you give an important message to your children. It means you no longer treat them as infants. You respect them as responsible citizens of your family.

Payment for Chores?

Not to my way of thinking. There are two schools of thought about why one gives a child an allowance. One group of experts say that the allowance is "payment" for chores and suggest you "fine" the child if chores are not done. The other group tells parents not to tie chores to allowances.

I feel quite strongly that we give our children allowances because they live in a complex world where money is important and they must learn money management.

But chores are something we all have to do. Chores are done in exchange for the privilege of living in a family home. Children should start doing chores almost from babyhood, whereas allowances make no sense until much later.

To my way of thinking, allowances are a right; chores are a responsibility and I prefer to separate them. You can, however, pay your child for "extraordinary" tasks around the house like cleaning the garage or painting. If you would have to hire a stranger, why not pay your child?

Money

ParenTips:

- *Start Early to Teach about Money.*

- *Do Not Tie Allowances to Chores.*

- *Make Allowance Rules Clear.*

- *Expect a Child to Save and Give to Charity.*

- *Use Money as an Incentive—But Judiciously.*

Start teaching children about money early because it's a complex issue and it takes a long time to teach and learn about it.

There are many things children have to learn about money: identifying coins and bills, counting, arithmetic, limits, priorities, values, saving accounts, check-writing, record-keeping, why we give money to those less fortunate, etc.

Basic Lessons

Let four-year-olds play with real coins and teach them how many coins make a dollar as soon as they can count.

Carry on a running commentary about what you are doing when shopping. "We have to put three quarters in the machine to get a drink." "The cereal and bananas cost $4.90, I get ten cents back." "I am paying for gasoline with a credit card."

Three-year-olds learn more about money when we hand them the money to make the transaction themselves. The commentary continues, "Here's a dollar so you can pay for the gum. Wait for the change. Let's count the change"

Five-year-olds identify coins and know that bills are identified by the big numbers on them. They can also count up to ten correctly. Some can add numbers up to their age with or without using their fingers. Let them take one or two items through the check-out line at a time when the store is not busy so they can practice giving money and getting change.

Explain to school-age children how credit cards and checks work. Take them with you to the store when you make a credit card purchase and to your desk when you write the check to pay for it.

Allowances

An allowance serves several purposes. First of all, an allowance will help teach your child what money is, what it does, that money can be saved, and that money you don't have can't be spent (at least not until you are grown-up and have a credit card!).

An allowance can also help your child develop autonomy, which means self-governance. When your child is young, you make the decisions about what your child eats and what toys your child plays with. As children get older, some of these decisions can and should be made by the children themselves.

Many, if not most, of the decisions we make involve money. An allowance enables you as parents to set up a practice field where, under your supervision, your children can begin to make decisions about what to buy.

It's important for children to feel that their parents trust them to make decisions on their own. Do not give extra money for items the child is supposed to purchase like lunch or your child might feel you don't have this trust and wonder why not. Because kids are egocentric, they will assume they did something wrong or aren't acting "big" enough.

Finally, allowances help teach children values: saving for the future, donating to those less fortunate, grappling with consumerism, resisting TV commercials.

I consider an allowance an "entitlement." Every child needs money in order to function in today's world. Until the child is grown and can earn money, the parents supply it just as they supply food and clothing.

I feel strongly that neither the amount or whether it is given for a particular period should be tied to the completion of chores. Chores are something we all have to do in exchange for the privilege of living in a home. Chores are a *respon-*

sibility; allowances are a *right*.

Although I am opposed to tying routine chores to the allowance, I have no objection to offering money for "extra" chores done well. What is an "extra" chore? Cleaning the garage or painting the porch, as opposed to making one's own bed every day. If you would pay a stranger to do the job, why not pay your child?

When should allowances be started? Most parents start allowances at about age six or when the child enters first grade.

How much should the allowance be? Just as parents do not give their children too much food, they should not give their children too much money—even if the parents are millionaires. Check with friends and neighbors to get the going rate, but make the final decision yourself.

A rule of thumb I have found useful is that you determine the amount of money you give the child by what the child's expenses are. For example, if the child has to purchase milk or lunch at school, the allowance should cover this plus a small sum that the adult world would call discretionary. The child can theoretically spend discretionary money the way he or she wants to.

But it is a good idea to keep some control over how the young child spends discretionary money. If your child has an allergy to chocolate you don't want the money to go for a candy bar. Ask the young child to check with you before making a purchase. When you realize the child has acceptable levels of judgment, remove this restriction and give the child the freedom to make his or her own decisions, including bad decisions, from which the child can learn.

Once you start the allowance, be careful not to give items or money to purchase items the child is supposed to purchase. If you do, you are negating the major teaching value of an allowance.

From the beginning expect your child to use a portion of the allowance for two purposes: **1)** save for the future and **2)** give to charity. Saving money for a future purchase and watching money accumulate serves as a counterweight to all the commercials calling for instant gratification spending.

Even first graders know about the homeless and the hungry they see on TV. Teach them to put a portion of their allowance aside to be added to the family contribution to a favorite charity.

As the child's expenses go up—with the need to purchase school supplies or sports paraphernalia—the allowance should be increased. I suggest raising the

CONTEMPORARY PARENTING PROBLEMS: Money

allowance at the beginning of every school year, as soon as you figure out what the child's responsibilities are.

Some parents extend the concept of the allowance to give teens a clothing allowance so they have the opportunity to learn how to make wise decisions about clothing purchases.

A family meeting is the perfect time to set down allowance rules. If the child should ask for something not on your shopping list when you are at the grocery store, say that must be purchased with his or her own money. You can, of course, buy what the child wants as a present or as a special treat.

This is also a good time to re-negotiate what the child should pay for. Birthday presents for friends? Clothes?

Saving Money

Teach children about saving money early on. The piggy bank is a good way to start but by age eight or so, open a savings account in the child's own name, although you will be the co-signer. The purpose of the savings account is to teach the child about interest payments and how to make wise decisions about using the money. Save it for college? Use it for a new bike?

Advanced Money Matters

As the children learn more arithmetic, involve them in making purchase deci-sions. Teach them about the large economy size. But also teach them that if you buy more than you need and it spoils, you are losing money.

When the family must make a big budget decision—shall we buy a new car or take a vacation—involve the children in the discussion. Show the children how you keep track of family finances, how you make out a budget, how you balance your checkbook. Talk about economic realities like inflation and interest rates.

I like to see responsible young teens, fourteen or so, assigned to actually write the household checks each month (you still sign) and balance the family check-book This is good practice that allows children to learn that running a household requires both money and good book-keeping practices.

I also like to see responsible sixteen-year-olds open their own checking accounts, which they must balance each month. This gets them ready for the real world of college or work. I told my children at that age that they were now responsible for buying their own clothes and put a suitable sum in their checking account at the beginning of the school year. They added birthday money or any wages earned to the account.

The Value of Money

Money not only has value but the way we spend money reflects our values. By involving children in monetary decisions made by the family they will learn about your family's values. When the children see that money that might be spent on a new car goes into the save-for-college fund, they see the way the family thinks about the future. They also learn about postponement of gratification for a future goal. All children today, who are bombarded with suggestions for instant gratification, need this lesson.

So children learn much more about the value of money from the way you **spend** your money than they will from what you **say about money.** Are you habitually overdrawn at the bank? Do you do a lot of impulse buying you later regret? Do you pay so much attention to the price that you ignore quality? Do you save regularly? Do you always give to charity?

I personally think it's important that children know about the family's financial situation. It is not necessary to tell a child exactly what your salary is, but it is important to tell of any impending change in finances ("Daddy may have to work extra hours so we can pay our bills," or "Mom was laid off from her job so we'll all have to watch what we are spending.")

During this lengthy process of teaching your children about money and values, give the child increasing autonomy and responsibility with each passing year. Your ultimate goal is to launch your children into the world able to manage money on their own when you are not around.

Remember that money decisions involve making choices and parents teach their children how to make choices in two ways. First, children watch how their parents make choices. Second, children make their own choices, under parental supervision at first. Wise parents empower their children by encouraging them to make choices and by refusing to rescue them from a bad choice.

Money as an Incentive

Money can be an appropriate incentive for children. As a matter of fact, anything legal that encourages children to do the right thing is OK in my book!

Some feel that both rewards and punishments control the child— rewards through "seduction" and punishment through pain—and that control undermines children's taking responsibility for making their own decisions.

But children are not born with the capacity to make wise decisions. They must learn how to do this. It's our job to teach these lessons. And just about all of us learn better with rewards than punishments.

Money can be an incentive once in a while, especially if it is for something the child really wants or for something the child is saving for. But avoid encouraging consumerism by using only money as an incentive.

Money makes our world go around. Never has it been more important for parents to teach children how to use money wisely, how to make proper purchasing decisions, how to evaluate the truth of commercials, how to save money for the future, and allocate a portion of their money to those less fortunate. All of these lessons start at home.

Epilogue

I hope that reading **ParenTips** has been helpful. My goal in writing the book was to provide parents with skills and strategies to help them deal with the common problems of contemporary parenthood. I don't have all the answers. And child development research hasn't even asked the right questions or designed appropriate research to find the answers.

So we—parents as well as advice-givers—muddle through the best we can. I guess my philosophy of parenting (and life) can be summed up as follows. I'm a pragmatist who tries to do what works, do as little harm as possible, act as kindly as I can to those I love and am responsible for, and accept the imperfections of every human being including myself.

I apologize to any parent who thinks I'm a wise-acre, know-it-all. Yes, I have tried to make things simple for my busy reader but parenting is NOT simple. We all struggle with the parenting process and we all have bad days. Nothing I have taught you will work all the time. Also, dealing with the so-called "difficult child" is beyond the scope of this book so there are parents out there who need much more than I can offer. Finally, I welcome questions, comments, and suggestions from parents or those who work with children. Please write to me care of the publisher:

Development Publications
P. O. Box 36748
Tucson, Arizona 85740

Suggested Further Readings

The following books have been useful to me in my work, or parents have told me about them, or both. Books that are out of print are labeled "library."

Child Care

American Academy of Pediatrics. **Caring for Your Baby and Young Child, Birth to Age 5.** New York: Bantam Books, 1998.

Useful information about basic child care and illnesses written mostly by pediatricians and put together by the American Academy of Pediatrics.

American Academy of Pediatrics. **Caring for Your School-age Child, Ages 5 to 12.** New York: Bantam Doubleday Dell Publishing Group, 1996.

Focus shifts to social and behavioral aspects of child-rearing with sections on family/ peer relationships and school.

Heins, Marilyn and Seiden, Anne. **Child Care/Parent Care.** New York: Doubleday, 1987 (library).

A comprehensive, commonsense child care book with an emphasis on taking care of yourselves as parents.

Leach, Penelope. **Your Baby and Child.** New York: Knopf, 1989.

Practical advice; good illustrations.

Leach, Penelope. **Your Growing Child.** New York: Knopf, 1986.

An encyclopedia of information about the care of children for those of you who like an a-to-z approach.

Spock, Benjamin and Parker, Steven. **Dr. Spock's Baby and Child Care.** New York: Pocket Books, 1998.

A classic. I have every edition of this book. What fascinates me is all the stuff that has never changed—much of Dr. Spock's approach and advice still holds!

Boston Children's Hospital Staff. **The New Child Health Encyclopedia.** New York: Dell, 1987 (library).

Useful information about illnesses in children.

Child Development and Temperament

Brazelton, T. Berry. **Touchpoints.** Reading, Massachusetts: Addison Wesley Longman, 1994.

A wordy but informative look at the development of young children.

Chess, Stella and Thomas, Alexander. **Know Your Child.** Northvale: Jason Aronson, 1996.

Lots I don't agree with, but these husband/wife psychiatrists clearly point out the importance of your child's temperament—and you ain't going to change it!

Gesell, Arnold. **The First Five Years of Life.** Cutchogue: Buccaneer Books, 1993.

Beautifully written, accurate observations of how our human babies grow and develop.

Gesell, Arnold. **The Child from Five to Ten.** New York: Harper and Row, 1946 (library).

Good descriptions of development in the school-age child.

Pulaski, Mary Ann. **Understanding Piaget.** New York: Harper & Row, 1980 (library).

This simplified Piaget is not exactly easy reading but it is informative—and fascinating.

Stallibrass, Alison. **The Self-Respecting Child.** Reading, Massachusetts: Addison-Wesley, 1989.

How spontaneous play is essential to child development.

Stoppard, Miriam. **Know Your Child.** New York: Ballantine, 1991.

One of my favorite gift books for new parents. Beautifully illustrated with photographs of babies and children doing what they are supposed to do at a given age.

Specific Issues

Faber, Adele and Mazlish, Elaine. **How To Talk So Kids Will Listen And Listen So Kids Will Talk.** New York: Avon Books, 1982.

A must for every parent. You can read this book in an hour and you will use the author's advice for a lifetime. It works for spouses, too!

Faber, Adele and Mazlish, Elaine. **Siblings Without Rivalry.** New York: Avon Books, 1988.

One of the books I wish was available when I was making all my parenting mistakes. Very sound advice on understanding and handling siblings.

Ferber, Richard. **Solve Your Child's Sleep Problems.** New York: Simon & Schuster, 1986.

Useful information about sleep including what parents can and can't do to get their kids to go to bed and stay there.

Galinsky, Ellen and David, Judy. **The Preschool Years.** New York: Ballantine Books, 1991.

A useful combination of parents' questions/observations/suggestions plus expert professional advice. I find myself taking this off the shelf over and over again—and I always find helpful information.

Garber, Stephen; Daniels, Marianne; Spizman, Robyn. **If Your Child Is Hyperactive, Inattentive, Impulsive, Distractible–.** New York: Random House, 1990.

Much practical information about attention deficit hyperactivity disorder–and how to parent a child who has it.

Garber, Stephen; Garber, Marianne; Spizman, Robyn. **Monsters Under The Bed and Other Childhood Fears.** New York: Random House, 1993.
Puts childhood fears into a developmental perspective and describes useful techniques for dealing with them.

Gordon, Thomas. **Teaching Children Self-Discipline—at Home and at School.** New York: Random House. 1989.
Helpful strategies for parents who haven't figured out how to be in charge and like it.

Gordon, Sol and Gordon, Judith. **Raising A Child Conservatively In A Sexually Permissive World.** New York: Simon & Schuster, 1984 (library).
One of my favorite sex education books. The Gordons understand the issues including how difficult it is for most parents to talk about sex.

Levine, Katherine. **When Good Kids Do Bad Things.** New York: Pocket Books, 1993.
Some useful suggestions for dealing with those awful things older kids do from wearing nose rings to hooking up with the wrong friends.

Marston, Stephanie. **The Magic of Encouragement.** New York: Morrow, 1990 (library).
Ways to parent–and even discipline—while helping your kids feel good about themselves.

Sammons, William. **I Wanna Do It Myself.** New York: Hyperion, 1992 library).
How toddlers achieve independence and why parents must learn to let them.

Stoppard, Miriam. **Questions Children Ask.** New York: DK Publishing, 1997.
No house with children should be without a copy of this marvelous book that helps parents face those tough questions all children ask. Suggested answers are divided into age groups because what we say to a child about, say, sex or death depends on the child's age/development.

Learning/School

Healy, Jane. **Endangered Minds.** New York: Simon and Schuster, 1991.

A guided trip through the brains and minds of children with a cautionary look at how today's children may be at a disadvantage.

Pinker, Steven. **The Language Instinct.** New York: William Morrow, 1994.

One of my favorite books. The story of how the human mind creates language written in language anyone can understand.

Rich, Dorothy. **MegaSkills.** New York: Houghton Mifflin, 1988.

How parents can help their children grow up and learn by instilling basic "MegaSkills" like confidence, initiative, and common sense.

Winner, Ellen. **Gifted Children.** New York: Basic Books, 1997.

Useful reading for parents who have, or think they may have, a gifted child.

Parenting and Families in Today's World

Chira, Susan. **A Mother's Place.** New York: HarperCollins, 1998.

A rational look at the debate about working mothers that should go a long way toward eliminating unnecessary guilt.

Harris, Judith. **The Nurture Assumption.** New York: The Free Press, 1998.

A wonderfully readable book that debunks many contemporary parenting myths.

Holcomb, Betty. **Not Guilty!** New York: Scribner, 1998.

Good news about working mothers–for a change!

Peters, Joan. **When Mothers Work.** Reading, Massachusetts: Addison-Wesley, 1997.

Another myth-buster about working mothers.

Pipher, Mary. **The Shelter of Each Other.** New York: Ballantine Books, 1996.

The real meaning of "family" and "community" lovingly outlined by a therapist who understands the importance of both.

Index

Development Publications

Mission and Concept

The mission of Development Publications is to create, prepare and distribute resources that focus on positive and constructive approaches to community and personal change. We address the major issues facing institutions, communities, organizations and individuals in today's world, building upon our extensive experience in the realms of community and personal development.

The Development Publications approach is one of community development and emphasizes the creation of conditions that promote the well-being of people. We encourage the belief that people are valuable resources who have significant contributions to make to their community. We emphasize the importance of diversity and its enormous potential to contribute to the processes of building and healing. Special importance is placed on the *local* community. Local events are seen as deeply related to global events, and both are viewed as interrelated parts of a holographic reality. We seek to encourage and give meaning to a compassionate society in which apparent antagonistic forces can become starting points for transformational community-building work. We are committed to confronting discrimination in its various forms and fostering an appreciation of the worth of every person. We believe in experiential approaches to lifelong learning, to building learning communities and to the creation of resources which foster learning. We recognize the differences between incremental and fundamental change, and promote fundamental change where it is needed for community development.

Development Publications seeks to become a significant creator, producer and distributor of resource materials that foster the pursuit of community, peace and justice.

William A. Lofquist
Publisher

For additional information contact: Development Publications, LLC
P. O. Box 36748
Tucson, Arizona 85740
Telephone: (520) 575-7047
FAX: (520) 575-8586
email: wlofquist@aol.com

ON THE SERENDIPITY ROAD: Exploring the Unexpected, by James R. Hine and Wayne F. Peate,MD. Paperback, 6x9 inches, 156 pages. $17.95

YOUNGER VOICES – STRONGER CHOICES: Promise Project's Guide to Forming Youth/Adult Partnerships, by Loring Leifer and Michael McLarney. Paperback, 8.5x11 inches, 84 pages. $14.95

TAKING CHARGE CONSTRUCTIVELY: A Framework for Personal Empowerment, by Dwight E. Palmer, Ph.D. Paperback, 6x9 inches, 198 pages. $17.95

DISCOVERING THE MEANING OF PREVENTION: A Practical Approach to Positive Change, by William A. Lofquist. Paperback, 6x9 inches, 151 pages. $17.95

THE PREVENTION DIMENSION: A Professional Development Game, created by William A. Lofquist and David Lynn. $29.95

THE TECHNOLOGY OF DEVELOPMENT: A Framework for Transforming Community Cultures, by William A. Lofquist. Paperback, 8.5x11 inches, 24 pages. $3.95

BREAKAWAY: A Framework for Creating Positive Drug- and Violence-Free School Communities, by David D. Lynn and William A. Lofquist. Paperback, 8.5x11 inches, 36 pages. $3.95

THE YOUTH OPPORTUNITY PLANNING PROCESS: A Systematic Approach to Involving Community Groups in Strategic Planning, by William A. Lofquist. Paperback, 8.5x11, 20 pages. $3.95

CREATING HEALTHY COMMUNITIES: An Audio-cassette Program that Introduces The Technology of Prevention, by William A. Lofquist. $19.95